MULTIPLE INTEGRALS

LIBRARY OF MATHEMATICS

edited by

WALTER LEDERMANN

D.Sc., Ph.D., F.R.S.Ed., Professor of
Mathematics, University of Sussex

MULTIPLE INTEGRALS

BY
WALTER LEDERMANN

LONDON: Routledge & Kegan Paul Ltd
NEW YORK: Dover Publications Inc

First published 1966
in Great Britain by
Routledge & Kegan Paul Ltd
Broadway House, 68–74 Carter Lane
London, E.C.4
and in the U.S.A. by
Dover Publications Inc.
180 Varick Street
New York, 10014

Library of Congress Catalog
Card Number 66–21244

Printed in Great Britain
by Butler & Tanner Ltd
Frome and London

36036

Preface

The aim of this book is to give an elementary treatment of multiple integrals. The notions of integrals extended over a curve, a plane region, a surface and a solid are introduced in turn, and methods for evaluating these integrals are presented in detail. Especial reference is made to the results required in Physics and other mathematical sciences, in which multiple integrals are an indispensable tool.

A full theoretical discussion of this topic would involve deep problems of analysis and topology, which are outside the scope of this volume, and concessions had to be made in respect of completeness without, it is hoped, impairing precision and a reasonable standard of rigour. As in the author's *Integral Calculus* (in this series), the main existence theorems are first explained informally and then stated exactly, but not proved. Topological difficulties are circumvented by imposing somewhat stringent, though no unrealistic, restrictions on the regions of integration.

Numerous examples are worked out in the text, and each chapter is followed by a set of exercises.

My thanks are due to my colleague Dr. S. Swierczkowski, who read the manuscript and made valuable suggestions.

W. LEDERMANN

The University of Sussex,
Brighton.

Contents

CHAPTER ONE
Line Integrals

1. PRELIMINARY REMARKS ABOUT CURVES

If $\phi(t)$ and $\psi(t)$ are continuous functions of t, defined in an interval $\alpha \leqslant t \leqslant \beta$, the equations

$$x = \phi(t), y = \psi(t) \qquad (\alpha \leqslant t \leqslant \beta) \qquad (1)$$

determine a *path* in the (x,y)-plane. We may think of t as the time and interpret (1) as the motion of a point whose coordinates at time t are $(\phi(t), \psi(t))$. For brevity, we often refer to this point as the point t of the path. The initial point and the end point of the path are $A = (\phi(\alpha), \psi(\alpha))$ and $B = (\phi(\beta), \psi(\beta))$ respectively. For a closed path, or *loop*, we have that

$$\phi(\alpha) = \phi(\beta), \psi(\alpha) = \psi(\beta).$$

In most cases the functions ϕ and ψ are not only continuous but possess continuous derivatives, except at a finite number of points. It may, however, be necessary to employ separate formulae to describe different sections of the path. For example, the path presented in Fig. 1 is defined as follows:

$$x = \begin{cases} t & (0 \leqslant t \leqslant 1) \\ 1 & (1 \leqslant t \leqslant 2) \\ 1 + \sin\dfrac{\pi}{2}(t-2) & (2 \leqslant t \leqslant 3) \end{cases}$$

$$y = \begin{cases} t & (0 \leqslant t \leqslant 2) \\ 3 - \cos\dfrac{\pi}{2}(t-2) & (2 \leqslant t \leqslant 3). \end{cases}$$

1

LINE INTEGRALS

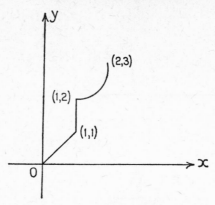

Figure 1.

The *curve* which constitutes the geometrical picture of the path is sometimes called the *track* of the path, but we observe that the equations (1) not only specify the curve but also indicate the sense and 'speed' with which the point traverses the curve. Thus, if $t_1 < t_2$, the point t_1 precedes the point t_2. If we are interested in the curve rather than in the path, we say that (1) gives a parametric representation of the curve, the variable t being called the parameter.

It should be noted that a given curve possesses many parametric equations. For example, each of the two pairs of equations

$$\text{(i) } x = \cos \pi t, \ y = \sin \pi t \qquad (0 \leqslant t \leqslant 1)$$

$$\text{(ii) } x = \frac{1-u^2}{1+u^2}, y = \frac{2u}{1+u^2} \qquad (0 \leqslant u \leqslant \infty)$$

represents the semi-circle in the upper half-plane starting at $(1,0)$ and ending at $(-1,0)$ (in (ii) the end-point corresponds to $u = \infty$). Thus (i) and (ii) are distinct paths which correspond to the

2

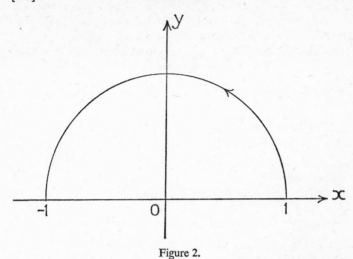

Figure 2.

same curve. However, we observe that in both cases the point describes the curve in the same sense, starting at (1,0) and terminating at (−1,0). In what follows we are chiefly concerned with curves having a given sense of description, the 'speed' being irrelevant for our purpose. We shall use the term '*orbit*' to denote a directed curve. Thus we may change the original parameter t by a sense-preserving transformation

$$t = h(u), \qquad (a \leqslant u \leqslant b) \tag{2}$$

which means that h is a continuous and (strictly) monotone increasing function. In these circumstances, (2) can be inverted, that is we can solve for u, say

$$u = k(t) \qquad (\alpha \leqslant t \leqslant \beta).$$

In particular $\alpha = h(a)$, $a = k(\alpha)$, $\beta = h(b)$, $b = k(\beta)$. In terms of the parameter u the orbit is given by

$$x = \phi(h(u)) = \phi_1(u), \; y = \psi(h(u)) = \psi_1(u) \quad (a \leqslant u \leqslant b). \tag{3}$$

3

Usually, the function h is not only continuous but has a continuous derivative, except possibly at a finite number of points.* This derivative is then necessarily positive except at a finite number of points, where it might vanish.* It is often convenient to use as parameter the length of arc, s, measured from the initial point up to a typical point t. Assuming that the functions ϕ and ψ have continuous derivatives, we have the formula

$$s = h(t) = \int_\alpha^t \{(\phi'(z))^2 + (\psi'(z))^2\}^{\frac{1}{2}} dz.$$

Hence

$$\frac{ds}{dt} = (\phi'(z))^2 + (\psi'(z))^2 \geqslant 0,$$

which shows that this is an admissible transformation.

2. DEFINITION OF A CURVILINEAR INTEGRAL

We saw in Chapter I of *Integral Calculus*† that the notion of a single integral can be motivated by considering the problem of finding the mass of a non-uniform straight wire. It is natural to pose the analogous question when the wire is bent. In the first instance we confine ourselves to the case where the shape of the wire is an arc of a continuous plane curve AB, which may be a loop. We assume that the curve is given by (1) and that the density at the point t is $\rho(t)$, where ρ is a continuous function of t. Subdivide the wire into small sections by inserting points $P_1, P_2, \ldots, P_{n-1}$ between A and B, corresponding to the parameter values $t_1 < t_2 < \ldots < t_{n-1}$. For convenience we put $A = P_0$, $B = P_n$, $\alpha = t_0$, $\beta = t_n$. Denoting

* For the sake of brevity we shall sometimes omit the explicit mention of this qualification.

† By the present author published in this series. This book will henceforth be referred to as *IC*.

4

the length of the arc $P_{i-1}P_i$ by λ_i we have that

$$\lambda_i = \int_{t_{i-1}}^{t_i} \{(\phi'(z))^2 + (\psi'(z))^2\}^{\frac{1}{2}} dz.$$

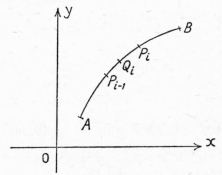

Figure 3.

On applying the Mean Value Theorem (*IC*, p. 7) we can write

$$\lambda_i = \{(\phi'(\tau_i))^2 + (\psi'(\tau_i))^2\}^{\frac{1}{2}}(t_i - t_{i-1}),$$

where τ_i is a certain number satisfying $t_{i-1} < \tau_i < t_i$. The parameter value τ_i corresponds to a point Q_i between P_{i-1} and P_i. Let the density at Q_i be $\rho_i = \rho(\tau_i)$. Then it is reasonable to take $\rho_i \lambda_i$ as an approximate value for the mass of the arc $P_{i-1}P_i$. The total mass of the wire is therefore approximately equal to

$$\sum_{i=1}^{n} \rho_i \lambda_i = \sum_{i=1}^{n} \rho(\tau_i)\{(\phi'(\tau_i))^2 + (\psi'(\tau_i))^2\}^{\frac{1}{2}}(t_i - t_{i-1}).$$

This is the kind of approximation sum which we considered in *IC*, p. 4. If we let the subdivision run through a set in which $\delta = \max(t_i - t_{i-1})$ tends to zero, then the sum tends to

$$M = \int_{\alpha}^{\beta} \rho(t)\{(\phi'(t))^2 + (\psi'(t))^2\}^{\frac{1}{2}} dt, \qquad (4)$$

which is an ordinary integral with respect to t. This, then, is the precise formula for the mass of the wire. The dependence on the particular parametric representation is only apparent. For let $t = h(u)$ be a sense-preserving transformation, as in (2) and (3). The foregoing argument would lead to an expression

$$M_1 = \int_a^b \rho_1(u)\{(\phi_1'(u))^2 + (\psi_1'(u))^2\}^{\frac{1}{2}}du$$

for the mass of the wire, where $\rho_1 = \rho(h(u))$ is the density in terms of u. However, $M_1 = M$, as is seen at once by changing the variable of integration from t to u in (4) and observing that

$$\{(\phi'(t))^2 + (\psi'(t))^2\}^{\frac{1}{2}} = \{(\phi_1'(u))^2 + (\psi_1'(u))^2\}^{\frac{1}{2}}\frac{du}{dt}.$$

The formula for M becomes especially simple and intuitively evident if we use s as parameter. Since

$$\frac{ds}{dt} = \{(\phi'(t))^2 + (\psi'(t))^2\}^{\frac{1}{2}},$$

we obtain that

$$M = \int_0^l \sigma(s)ds,$$

where l is the length of the curve and $\sigma(s)$ the expression of the density in terms of s.

We now turn to a different type of problem, which is of particular importance in Physics. First, we confine ourselves to a two-dimensional situation. Suppose a particle moving along the orbit (1) where t is the time, is subject to a force which varies along the orbit and at the point (x,y) is represented by the vector $\mathbf{F} = (p(x,y), q(x,y))$. Since we are concerned only with points on the curve, the components of $\mathbf{F}$ are effectively functions of t, thus

$$p(\phi(t), \psi(t)) = P(t), \qquad q(\phi(t), \psi(t)) = Q(t).$$

6

As is known from Mechanics, the rate of work done during the motion is

$$p\frac{dx}{dt} + q\frac{dy}{dt} = P(t)\phi'(t) + Q(t)\psi'(t) = R(t),$$

say.

Hence the total work is given by

$$W = \int_\alpha^\beta\left(p\frac{dx}{dt} + q\frac{dy}{dt}\right)dt = \int_\alpha^\beta R(t)dt, \qquad (5)$$

which is an ordinary integral with respect to t. It is important to note that the value of the integral does not depend on the particular parametrization of the orbit. For if we make an admissible transformation $t = h(u)$ and use u as variable of integration in (5) we find that

$$W = \int_a^b\left(p\frac{dx}{dt} + q\frac{dy}{dt}\right)\frac{dt}{du}du = \int_a^b\left(p\frac{dx}{du} + q\frac{dy}{du}\right)du,$$

which has the same form as (5), except that u has been used as parameter instead of t. It is therefore customary to suppress all mention of a parameter and to write the integral (5) in the form

$$W = \int_\Gamma p\,dx + q\,dy, \qquad (6)$$

where the symbol Γ refers to the orbit along which the integral is to be taken. It is understood that for an evaluation of this integral one has to choose a parametrization of Γ and thus reduce (6) to an ordinary integral (5). Integrals of the type (6) are called *line integrals* or *curvilinear integrals*. In a purely mathematical context, p and q need not be the components of a vector, and the integral exists provided that these functions and the curve satisfy suitable conditions of regularity.

We append the following formal rules concerning line integrals

7

LINE INTEGRALS

(1) *If Γ is composed of the two orbits Γ_1 and Γ_2, then*

$$\int_{\Gamma} = \int_{\Gamma_1} + \int_{\Gamma_2},$$

where the integrand in each case is $p(x,y)dx + q(x,y)dy$.

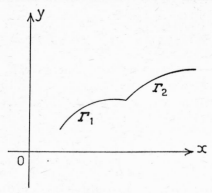

Figure 4.

(2) *If Γ' is the orbit opposite to Γ, that is the same curve described in the opposite sense, then*

$$\int_{\Gamma'} = -\int_{\Gamma}.$$

Example 1. Evaluate $\int_{\Delta} y^2dx + x^2dy$, where Δ is the boundary of the triangle with vertices $O = (0,0)$, $A = (1,0)$, $B = (0,1)$, described in this order (see Fig. 5).

The orbit consists of three sections, requiring separate choices of parameter.

(1) On OA we use x as parameter; hence OA is given by the

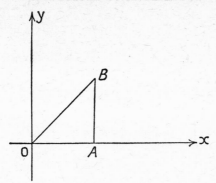

Figure 5.

pair of equations $x = x, y = 0$ $(0 \leqslant x \leqslant 1)$. Evidently $\dfrac{dy}{dx} = 0$ and

$$\int_{OA} = \int_0^1 \left(0\dfrac{dx}{dx} + x\dfrac{dy}{dx} \right) dx = 0.$$

(2) On AB we use y as parameter and represent this segment by

$$x = 1, y = y \qquad (0 \leqslant y \leqslant 1).$$

Hence

$$\int_{AB} = \int_0^1 \left(y^2\dfrac{dx}{dy} + x^2\dfrac{dy}{dy} \right) dy = \int_0^1 (y^2.0 + 1) dy = 1.$$

(3) On BO we put $x = t, y = t$, where t ranges from 1 to 0 (in this order). Hence

$$\int_{BO} = \int_1^0 \left(y^2\dfrac{dx}{dt} + x^2\dfrac{dy}{dt} \right) dt = -\int_0^1 (t^2 + t^2) dt = -\dfrac{2}{3}.$$

Combining these results we find that

$$\int_\Delta y^2 dx + x^2 dy = \dfrac{1}{3}.$$

Example 2. Evaluate the integrals (i) $\int_\Gamma y\, dx$ and (ii) $\int_\Gamma x\, dy$, where Γ is the circle $x^2 + y = a^2$ described in the counter-clockwise sense.

Parametrizing Γ by the equations $x = a \cos t$, $y = a \sin t$ $(0 \leqslant t \leqslant 2\pi)$ we obtain that

(i) $\displaystyle\int_\Gamma y\, dx = \int_0^{2\pi} y\frac{dx}{dt}dt = \int_0^{2\pi} a \sin t(-a \sin t)dt$

$$= -a^2 \int_0^{2\pi} \sin^2 t\, dt = -\pi a^2.$$

(ii) $\displaystyle\int_\Gamma x\, dy = \int_0^{2\pi} x\frac{dy}{dx}dt = \int_2^{2\pi} a \cos t\, a \cos t\, dt$

$$= a^2 \int_0^{2\pi} \cos^2 t\, dt = \pi a^2.$$

Example 3. For every closed curve Γ, $\displaystyle\int_\Gamma dx = \int_\Gamma dy = 0$.

For $\displaystyle\int_\Gamma dx = \int_\alpha^\beta \frac{d\phi}{dt}dt = \phi(\beta) - \phi(\alpha) = 0$. Similarly $\displaystyle\int_\Gamma dy = 0$.

The last example is a special case of a much more general situation. Assume that there exists a (single-valued) function f such that

$$p = f_x, \qquad q = f_y \tag{7}$$

where f_x and f_y are the partial derivatives of f with respect to x and y respectively. It is convenient to write $f(X)$ for $f(x,y)$, where X is the point (x,y). Now let Γ be a path from A to B, given by the equations (1). Then, on Γ, f is a function of t only and*

$$\frac{d}{dt}f = f_y\frac{dx}{dt} + f_x\frac{dy}{dt}.$$

---

* P. J. Hilton, *Partial Derivatives* in this series, Theorem 2.2, p. 12.

Hence

$$\int_\Gamma f_x dx + f_y dy = \int_\alpha^\beta \frac{df}{dt}dt = f(B) - f(A).$$

It is a remarkable fact that this result is independent of the path joining A and B. In particular, *if Γ is any closed path*

$$\int_\Gamma f_x dx + f_y dy = 0. \qquad (8)$$

On putting in turn $f = x$ and $f = y$ we obtain the formulae proved in Example 3.

We shall now briefly mention the extension to integrals which are associated with curves in three-dimensional space (twisted curves*). Such curves are parametrically represented by three equations

$$x = \phi(t), \; y = \psi(t), \; z = \chi(t) \qquad (\alpha \leqslant t \leqslant \beta).$$

As in the case of plane curves, two types of integral arise.

(i) If s is the arc of the curve, measured from its starting point, up to the point t, then

$$s = h(t) = \int_\alpha^t \{(\phi'(z))^2 + (\psi'(z))^2 + (\chi'(z))^2\}^{\frac{1}{2}} dz.$$

A typical integral with respect to the arc length is then

$$\int_\Gamma \rho(s) ds = \int_\alpha^\beta \rho(h(t)) \{(\phi'(t))^2 + (\psi'(t))^2 + (\chi'(t))^2\}^{\frac{1}{2}} dt,$$

where the integral on the right is an ordinary integral with respect to t.

(ii) A curvilinear integral of the form

$$W = \int_\Gamma p \, dx + q \, dy + r \, dz,$$

where p, q and r are arbitrary continuous functions of x, y and

* See K. L. Wardle, *Differential Geometry*, in this series, Chapter 2.

z is evaluated with the aid of the parametrization and becomes

$$W = \int_\alpha^\beta \left(p\frac{dx}{dt} + q\frac{dy}{dt} + r\frac{dz}{dt} \right)dt,$$

with the understanding that x, y and z are expressed in terms of t. As before, it is shown that the value does not depend on the choice of parameter.

3. AREA

On page 5 of *IC* we have alluded to the conceptional difficulties involved in defining the area of a region. It is not our intention to give a rigorous theory of area in this book, and we shall be satisfied with a treatment of area which suffices for simple regions. Basically, we adopt the view that area can be defined in terms of integrals, although the opposite procedure is also possible and indeed seems to be more natural. We recall the elementary case of a region A_0 which is bounded by a finite segment $[a,b]$ on the x-axis, the vertical lines $x = a$, $x = b$ and the arc of a continuous curve $y = f(x)$, where $f(x) \geqslant 0$ when $a \leqslant x \leqslant b$ (see Fig. 6).

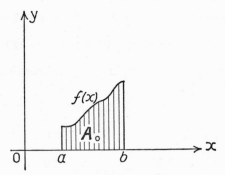

Figure 6.

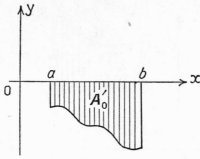

Figure 7.

Adopting the general notation $|A|$ for the area of A we have that

$$|A_0| = \int_a^b f(x)dx.$$

We regard area as an essentially non-negative number. Hence if the arc of the curve lies below the x-axis, that is if $f(x) \leqslant 0$ when $a \leqslant x \leqslant b$ the region A_0' shown in Fig. 7 has an area given by

$$|A_0'| = -\int_a^b f(x)dx,$$

and if the curve lies partly above and partly below the axis we have to use the general formula

$$|A| = \int_a^b |f(x)|dx.$$

It is now an easy step to define the area of a region A_1 that is comprised between two curves $y = f_1(x)$ and $y = f_2(x)$, where $f_1(x) \geqslant f_2(x)$, and the lines $x = a$, $x = b$ (see Fig. 8). Such a region is said to be *normal with respect to the x-axis*. It is clear that in this case

$$|A_1| = \int_a^b \{f_1(x) - f_2(x)\}dx. \tag{9}$$

13

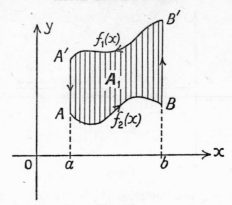

Figure 8.

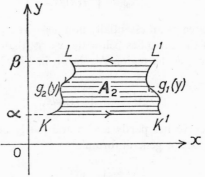

Figure 9.

We shall now demonstrate that this result can be expressed more concisely as a line integral taken along the boundary, Γ, of A_1. Here, and in the sequel, it will be assumed that Γ is described in the counter-clockwise sense, as indicated in Fig. 8.

Consider the line integral $\int_\Gamma y \, dx$. It is convenient to think of

14

Γ as being composed of four sections, namely $A'A$, AB, BB' and $B'A'$. Along the vertical segments, x is constant and therefore $dx/dt = 0$, whatever the parametrization; or, more shortly, $dx = 0$. Hence these sections make no contributions to the line integral. On the arc AB we can use x as parameter and use the parametrization $AB: x = x, y = f_2(x)\,(a \leqslant x \leqslant b)$.

Hence $\int_{AB} y\,dx = \int_a^b f_2(x)dx$. On the arc $B'A'$ we may also use x as parameter, thus $B'A': x = x, y = f_1(x)\ (b \geqslant x \geqslant a)$ bearing in mind the orientation. Hence

$$\int_{B'A'} y\,dx = \int_b^a f_1(x)dx = -\int_a^b f_1(x)dx.$$

Collecting these results we have that

$$\int_\Gamma y\,dx = \int_b^a \{f_2(x) - f_1(x)\}dx.$$

In view of (9) we may therefore state that if a *region* A_2 *is normal with respect to the x-axis, then its area is given by*

$$|A_2| = -\int_\Gamma y\,dx. \tag{10}$$

In a similar manner we can deal with regions, A_2, which are *normal with respect to the y-axis*. The boundary of such a region consists of two arcs $x = g_1(y)$ and $x = g_2(y)$ $(\alpha \leqslant y \leqslant \beta)$, subject to the condition $g_1(y) \geqslant g_2(y)$. By the rules of elementary integral calculus

$$|A_2| = \int_\alpha^\beta \{g_1(y) - g_2(y)\}dy. \tag{11}$$

Now consider the line integral $\int_\Gamma x\,dy$. No contribution comes from the horizontal segments KK' and $L'L$ (see Fig. 9) because

15

$dy = 0$ on these sections. Also, with due regard to orientation,

$$\int_{K'L'} x \, dy = \int_{\alpha}^{\beta} g_1(y) dy, \qquad \int_{LK} x \, dy = -\int_{\alpha}^{\beta} g_2(y) dy.$$

On adding these results and comparing with (11) we can assert that *if a region A_2 is normal with respect to the y-axis*,

$$|A_2| = \int_{\Gamma} x \, dy. \tag{12}$$

The difference in sign is a consequence of our convention about orientation.

A region, A, which is normal with respect to both axes will simply be called *normal*. In such a case, both (10) and (12) apply, and we can get a more symmetrical expression by adding these formulae and dividing by 2. Thus *if A is a normal region with boundary Γ*,

$$|A| = \tfrac{1}{2} \int_{\Gamma} x \, dy - y \, dx, \tag{13}$$

or in terms of the parametric representation (1)

$$|A| = \tfrac{1}{2} \int_{\alpha}^{\beta} \left(x \frac{dy}{dt} - y \frac{dx}{dt} \right) dt.$$

Although we have derived (13) only for normal regions, the right-hand side of the equation is evidently meaningful for a much wider class of regions. We might therefore use (13) to *define* the area for a region whose boundary is any simple closed curve, that is a continuous curve with no self-intersection, having a parametric representation which renders the line integral valid. Whilst this definition suffices to evaluate the area in most practical cases, it is not suitable for an adequate theory* of area. Such a theory is outside the scope

---

* See e.g. W. W. Rogosinski, *Volume and Integral* (University Mathematical Texts, Oliver and Boyd).

of this book; but whenever necessary, we shall use, without proof, such general propositions as:

(1) If the regions A and B have definite areas, so have their union A ∪ B and their intersection A ∩ B.

(2) If A and B have no interior points in common, then

$$|A \cup B| = |A| + |B|.$$

Since the area of a region does not depend on the choice of coordinate axes, we expect that the formulae (10), (12) and (13) are unchanged when we introduce a new frame of reference by making the transformation

$$x = a + \xi \cos \alpha + \eta \sin \alpha,$$
$$y = b - \xi \sin \alpha + \eta \cos \alpha, \quad (14)$$

where (a,b) is the new origin and (ξ,η) are the new coordinates.

Let us verify the invariance of the integral (12). Using (14) for the points on Γ we must regard ξ and η as functions of t, corresponding to the parametric equations (1). Thus

$$x \, dy = (a + \xi \cos \alpha + \eta \sin \alpha)(-\sin \alpha \, d\xi + \cos \alpha \, d\eta).$$

When integrating this expression over the closed contour Γ we observe that

$$\int_\Gamma d\xi = \int_\Gamma d\eta = \int_\Gamma \xi d\xi = \int_\Gamma \eta d\eta = \int_\Gamma \xi d\eta + \eta d\xi = 0,$$

the last three results being instances of ((8), p. 11) with f equal to $\frac{1}{2}\xi^2$ or $\frac{1}{2}\eta^2$ or $\xi\eta$ respectively. On expanding and collecting terms we find that

$$\int_\Gamma x \, dy = \cos^2\alpha \int_\Gamma \xi d\eta - \sin^2\alpha \int_\Gamma \eta d\xi = \int_\Gamma \xi d\eta,$$

which proves the invariance of (12), because

$$\int_\Gamma \eta d\xi = -\int_\Gamma \xi d\eta.$$

17

LINE INTEGRALS

Example 4. To find the area of the circle $x^2 + y^2 = a^2$ we use the parametric equations $x = a \cos t$, $y = a \sin t$ $(0 \leqslant t \leqslant 2\pi)$. Hence the area is

$$\tfrac{1}{2}\int_0^{2\pi} (xy' - yx')dt = \tfrac{1}{2}a^2 \int_0^{2\pi} (\cos^2 t + \sin^2 t)dt = \pi a^2.$$

Example 5. The *astroid* is the star-shaped curve shown in Fig. 10.

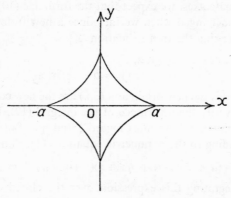

Figure 10.

It has the parametric representation

$$x = a \cos^3 t, \; y = a \sin^3 t \qquad (0 \leqslant t \leqslant 2\pi).$$

The area enclosed by the curve is

$$\tfrac{1}{2}\int_0^{2\pi} (xy' - yx')dt = \frac{3a^2}{2}\int_0^{2\pi} (\cos^4 t \sin^2 t + \sin^4 t \cos^2 t)dt$$

$$= \frac{3a^2}{2}\int_0^{2\pi} \cos^2 t \sin^2 t \, dt = \frac{3a^2}{8}\int_0^{2\pi} \sin^2 2t \, dt$$

$$= \frac{3a^2}{8}\int_0^{2\pi} (\tfrac{1}{2} - \tfrac{1}{2}\cos 4t)dt = \frac{3a^2}{16}.$$

18

In some problems the boundary of a region is expressed in terms of polar coordinates, so that its equation is

$$r = f(\theta) \qquad (\kappa \leqslant \theta \leqslant \lambda). \qquad (15)$$

More generally, we may suppose that both r and θ are functions of a parameter t, say

$$r = p(t), \quad \theta = q(t) \qquad (\alpha \leqslant t \leqslant \beta). \qquad (16)$$

In order to adapt the formula for the area to this case we use the relations $x = r \cos \theta$, $y = r \sin \theta$, where r and θ must now be regarded as functions of t in accordance with (16). It follows that

$$x' = r' \cos \theta - r \sin \theta \, \theta', \, y' = r' \sin \theta + r \cos \theta \, \theta',$$

whence, after a short calculation,

$$xy' - yx' = r^2\theta'.$$

Hence the formula for the area becomes

$$|A| = \tfrac{1}{2} \int_\alpha^\beta r^2\theta' dt. \qquad (17)$$

When θ is itself the parameter, as in (15), we find that

$$|A| = \tfrac{1}{2} \int_\kappa^\lambda r^2 d\theta.$$

Example 6. The *Lemniscate* (Fig. 11) has the equation $r^2 = a^2 \cos 2\theta$, which yields real values for r only when $-\pi/4 \leqslant \theta \leqslant \pi/4$ and $3\pi/4 \leqslant \theta \leqslant 5\pi/4$.

The curve consists of two loops joined at the origin. The total area is twice the area of each loop and is given by

$$\int_{-\pi/4}^{\pi/4} r^2 d\theta = a^2 \int_{-\pi/4}^{\pi/4} \cos 2\theta d\theta = a^2.$$

LINE INTEGRALS

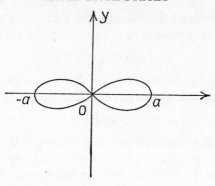

Figure 11.

EXERCISES ON CHAPTER ONE

1. Find parametric equations for the arc of the curve $y^2 = x^3$ (1, -1) to (1,1) (via O).

2. Obtain parametric equations for the closed curve consisting of the arc of the parabola $y^2 = x$ between $(-1, 1)$ and (1,1) and the chord joining these points, where the parameter ranges from -1 to 2.

3. Evaluate $\int_\Gamma y \, ds$, where Γ is the arc of the curve $y^2 = x$ from (0,0) to (1,1).

4. Find $\int_\Gamma \dfrac{dx + dy}{(x^2 + y^2)^{1/2}}$, where Γ is the circumference of the square: $-1 \leqslant x, y \leqslant 1$.

5. Evaluate $\int_\Gamma \dfrac{dx - dy}{x + y + 1}$, where Γ is the circumference of the triangle $x > 0$, $y > 0$, $x + y \leqslant 1$.

6. Prove that if $p(x)$ and $q(y)$ are continuous functions of x and y respectively and Γ is any loop, then $\int_\Gamma p \, dx + q \, dy = 0$.

EXERCISES

7. Show that if Γ is the circumference of the circle $x = a \cos t$, $y = a \sin t$ $(0 \leqslant t \leqslant 2\pi)$, then $\displaystyle\int_\Gamma \frac{x\,dy - y\,dx}{x^2 + y^2} = 2\pi$.

8. Note that, in the preceding problem, $\dfrac{-y}{x^2 + y^2} = \dfrac{\partial}{\partial x} \tan^{-1}\left(\dfrac{y}{x}\right)$, $\dfrac{x}{x^2 + y^2} = \dfrac{\partial}{\partial y} \tan^{-1}\left(\dfrac{y}{x}\right)$. Why is the integral not equal to zero in virtue of (8), p. 11?

9. Evaluate $\displaystyle\int_\Gamma x\,dy - y\,dx + z\,dz$, where Γ is the portion of the *helix* given by $x = a \cos t$, $y = a \sin t$, $x = bt$ $(0 \leqslant t \leqslant 2\pi)$.

10. Prove that the area of the *cardioid* $r = a(1 - \cos \theta)$ $(0 \leqslant \theta \leqslant 2\pi)$ is $\dfrac{3}{2}\pi a^2$.

11. Show that if $AB > H^2$, $\displaystyle\int_\Gamma \frac{x\,dy - y\,dx}{Ax^2 + 2Hxy + By^2} = 2\sigma$, where Γ is the circle $x^2 + y^2 = a^2$ and σ is the area enclosed by the ellipse $Ax^2 + 2Hxy + By^2 = 1$.

12. Sketch the curve $x = a \sin 2t$, $y = b \cos t$ $(0 \leqslant t \leqslant 2\pi)$ and find the area of either loop.

CHAPTER TWO
Double Integrals

1. DEFINITION OF A DOUBLE INTEGRAL

We start by considering the two-dimensional analogue of finding the mass of a non-uniform wire. We now have a lamina of material which covers a finite region D of the (x,y)-plane and whose density at (x,y) is $f(x,y)$. In order to obtain

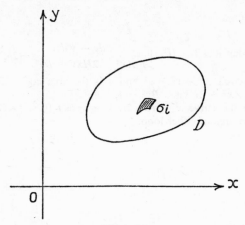

Figure 12.

an approximation to the total mass of the lamina we divide D into small partial regions by a *partition*

$$\Delta: \sigma_1, \sigma_2, \ldots, \sigma_n \tag{1}$$

and select a point $(x_i.y_i)$ in σ_i $(i = 1, 2, \ldots, n)$. The mass of each fragment is then approximately $f(x_i, y_i)|\sigma_i|$, where $|\sigma_i|$ is the area of σ_i. The total mass is given approximately by

$$S(\Delta) = \sum_{i=1}^{n} f(x_i, y_i)|\sigma_i|,$$

which we shall call the *approximation sum* associated with the partition Δ. We say Δ is of *norm* v if every σ_i of Δ can be enclosed in a disc of radius v, but not every σ_i can be enclosed in a disc of radius less than v. It can then be shown that, under suitable conditions on f and D, the sum $S(\Delta)$ tends to a finite limit as $v \rightarrow 0$. This limit is denoted by

$$\iint_D f(x,y)dxdy$$

and is called the *double integral* of f over D. For a proof of this fundamental existence theorem the reader must be referred to more advanced books.* It will be understood that the theorem can be established only under reasonable conditions on f and D. For our purposes it suffices to assume that f is bounded and continuous in D, except possibly on a finite number of arcs lying in D. Furthermore, the region D is finite and is bounded by a finite number of arcs. Each arc can be parametrically represented by equations $x = \phi(t), y = \psi(t)$, in which ϕ and ψ are continuous functions having continuous derivatives, except possibly at a finite number of points. In order to avoid awkward complications we shall stipulate that ϕ' and ψ' have at most a finite number of zeros. Regions which satisfy these conditions may be described as '*sectionally smooth*'. We may then summarize the basic existence theorem as follows.

Existence Theorem. Let D be a sectionally smooth region in

* R. Courant, *Differential and Integral Calculus*, vol. II, Chapter 4 (Blackie and Son), where a somewhat different approach is used.

the (x,y)-plane. Assume that the function f is bounded throughout D and continuous in D, except possibly on a finite number of simple arcs lying in D. Let

$$\Delta: \sigma_1, \sigma_2, \ldots, \sigma_n$$

be a partition of D with norm v. In each σ_i choose a point (x_i, y_i) $(i = 1, 2, \ldots, n)$ and form the approximation sum

$$S(\Delta) = \sum_{i=1}^{n} f(x_i, y_i)|\sigma_i|. \tag{2}$$

Then, as $v \longrightarrow 0$, $S(\Delta)$ tends to a finite limit, which is denoted by

$$\iint_D f(x,y)dxdy.$$

This limit is independent of the shape of the partial regions σ_i and of the choice of (x_i, y_i) in σ_i.

Remarks. The notion of a double integral must be clearly distinguished from that of a repeated integral (*IC*, p. 33), although the two concepts are closely related, as will be demonstrated in the next section. Double integration is essentially a two-dimensional operation, and $\iint$ must be regarded as a single symbol. The traditional notation *dxdy* stems from the fact that, if D is broken up by a rectangular grating (see Fig. 13), a typical partial region is a 'small' rectangle of area $|\sigma| = dxdy$. Again, this notation is symbolical and some authors prefer to use a single 'differential' such as $d\sigma$ in place of *dxdy*. This point will be further elucidated later (p. 52).

We shall now state some general properties of double integrals, which are straightforward consequences of the definition.

(i) $$\iint_D dxdy = |D| \ (= \text{area of } D).$$

24

[2.1] DEFINITION OF A DOUBLE INTEGRAL

This follows by considering the mass of a uniform lamina of density equal to unity.

(ii) $\displaystyle\iint_D (f+g)\,dxdy = \iint_D f\,dxdy + \iint_D g\,dxdy.$

(iii) If c is a constant, $\displaystyle\iint_D cf\,dxdy = c\iint_D f\,dxdy.$

(iv) If the regions D_1 and D_2 have no interior point in common,

$$\iint_{D_1} f\,dxdy + \iint_{D_2} f\,dxdy = \iint_D f\,dxdy,$$

where $D = D_1 \cup D_2$ is the union of D_1 and D_2.

(v) If $f \leqslant g$ for all points of D, then this inequality may be integrated, thus

$$\iint_D f\,dxdy \leqslant \iint_D g\,dxdy.$$

In particular, if m and M are constants such that $m \leqslant f \leqslant M$ holds throughout D, then on integrating over D we obtain that

$$m|D| \leqslant \iint_D f\,dxdy \leqslant M|D|. \tag{3}$$

Again, by integrating the obvious inequalities $-|f| \leqslant f \leqslant |f|$ we find that

$$-\iint_D |f|\,dxdy \leqslant \iint_D f\,dxdy \leqslant \iint_D |f|\,dxdy,$$

which can be more briefly expressed as

$$\left|\iint_D f\,dxdy\right| \leqslant \iint_D |f|\,dxdy. \tag{4}$$

Let us now assume that f is continuous throughout D. We may then take for m and M the least and the greatest value respectively which f attains in D. The inequalities (3) state that

25

$|D|^{-1}\iint_D f\,dxdy$ lies between these two values. It is known that a continuous function attains every value between m and M, that is there exists at least one point (ξ,η) in D such that $|D|^{-1}\iint_D f\,dxdy = f(\xi,\eta)$. This is an important result, which is usually referred to as the

Mean Value Theorem. If f is continuous in D, there exists at least one point (ξ,η) in D such that

$$\iint_D f\,dxdy = f(\xi,\eta)|D|. \tag{5}$$

2. DOUBLE INTEGRALS OVER A RECTANGLE

The Existence Theorem given in the preceding section does not lead to a method of evaluating double integrals, except in very rare circumstances. In most concrete cases one uses a procedure which makes it possible to reduce the double integral to a repeated integral, that is to two ordinary integrals carried out in succession, one variable being kept constant initially.

We begin with the simplest case, in which the region of integration is a (finite) rectangle, and we shall assume in the first instance that $f(x,y)$ is continuous throughout R.

Theorem 1. If f is continuous in the rectangle

$$R: a \leqslant x \leqslant b, \alpha \leqslant y \leqslant \beta,$$

then

$$\iint_R f(x,y)dxdy = \int_a^b dx \int_\alpha^\beta f(x,y)dy = \int_\alpha^\beta dy \int_a^b f(x,y)dx. \tag{6}$$

Proof. In order to apply the definition of the double integral described in the Existence Theorem (p. 23) we break up R by

separately subdividing the ranges for x and y and then drawing
vertical and horizontal lines through the points of subdivision.
Thus the partitioning, Δ, of R is specified by the inequalities

$$\Delta: \begin{cases} a = x_0 < x_1 < \ldots < x_{m-1} < x_m = b \\ \alpha = y_0 < y_1 < \ldots < y_{n-1} < y_n = \beta \end{cases}$$

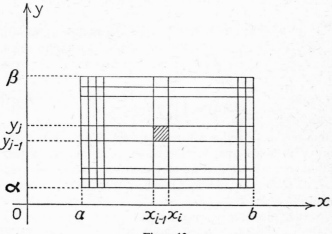

Figure 13.

This determines a network in which a typical rectangular mesh
is given by

$$\rho_{ij}: \begin{cases} x_{i-1} \leqslant x \leqslant x_i \\ y_{j-1} \leqslant y \leqslant y_j \end{cases} \quad (i = 1, 2, \ldots, m; j = 1, 2, \ldots, n).$$

Clearly, it is convenient in this case to label the subregions by a
double suffix, and we have therefore written ρ_{ij} instead of the
σ_i which occurred in (1). Since ρ_{ij} can be enclosed in a disc
of radius $\frac{1}{2}\{(x_i - x_{i-1})^2 + (y_j - y_{j-1})^2\}^{\frac{1}{2}}$, it follows that the
norm of Δ is given by

$$\nu = \max_{i,j} \tfrac{1}{2}\{(x_i - x_{i-1})^2 + (y_j - y_{j-1})^2\}^{\frac{1}{2}}. \tag{7}$$

The choice of an arbitrary point (ξ_{ij}, η_{ij}) in ρ_{ij} is conveniently accomplished by selecting arbitrary points ξ_i and η_j in $[x_{i-1}, x_i]$ and $[y_{j-1}, y_j]$ respectively and then putting $(\xi_{ij}, \eta_{ii}) = (\xi_i, \eta_j)$. Thus we form the approximation sum

$$S(\Delta) = \sum_{i=1}^{m} \sum_{j=1}^{n} f(\xi_i, \eta_j)(x_i - x_{i-1})(y_j - y_{j-1}),$$

and we know that $S(\Delta)$ can be made to lie as close as we wish to the double integral, provided only that ν is sufficiently small. More precisely, if ε is an arbitrary positive number, we can find $\nu(=\nu(\varepsilon))$ such that

$$\left| S(\Delta) - \iint_R f \, dx dy \right| < \varepsilon. \tag{8}$$

From now on ε and ν will remain fixed. We recall that this inequality holds whatever the choice of ξ_i and η_j in their respective intervals, and we may therefore postpone the precise determination of these numbers to a more opportune moment.

Next consider the repeated integral

$$\int_a^b dx \int_\alpha^\beta f(x,y) dy = \int_a^b F(x) dx.$$

It is known that

$$F(x) = \int_\alpha^\beta f(x,y) dy \tag{9}$$

is a continuous function. (This was proved in *IC*, p. 28, under an additional condition, which however can be removed by using more advanced arguments.) Breaking up the range of integration for x we can write

$$\int_a^b F(x) dx = \sum_{i=1}^{n} \int_{x_{i-1}}^{x_i} F(x) dx. \tag{10}$$

By the Mean Value Theorem of the integral calculus (*IC*, p. 7, equation (11)), there exists a number ξ_i in $[x_{i-1}, x_i]$ such that

$$\int_{x_{i-1}}^{x_i} F(x)dx = F(\xi_i)(x_i - x_{i-1}), \tag{11}$$

and we shall use this ξ_i for the formation of $S(\Delta)$. Keeping i fixed we have that

$$F(\xi_i) = \int_{\alpha}^{\beta} f(\xi_i, y)dy = \sum_{j=1}^{n} \int_{y_{j-1}}^{y_j} f(\xi_i, y)dy$$
$$= \sum_{j=1}^{n} f(\xi_i, \eta_j)(y_j - y_j), \tag{12}$$

where η_j is a certain number in $[y_{j-1}, y_j]$ whose existence is guaranteed by the Mean Value Theorem. This η_j is our choice for $S(\Delta)$. Substituting first (11) and then (12) in (10) we find that

$$\int_{a}^{b} F(x)dx = \sum_{i=1}^{m} \sum_{j=1}^{n} f(\xi_i, \eta_j)(x_i - x_{i-1})(y_j - y_j) = S(\Delta). \tag{13}$$

If we make the subdivision on the coordinate axes so fine that $\max\limits_{i,j} \{|x_i - x_{i-1}|, \; |y_j - y_{j-1}|\} < \nu\sqrt{2}$, the norm (7) of $S(\Delta)$ becomes less than ν, and by combining (8) and (13) we infer that

$$\left| \int_{a}^{b} F(x)dx - \int\int_{R} f(x,y)dxdy \right| < \varepsilon.$$

By the usual argument, we may conclude that the two numbers on the left are in fact equal. For if not, the absolute value of their difference would be a positive number p. On taking $\varepsilon = p$, as we may, we should arrive at a contradiction. Thus,

$$\int\int_{R} f(x,y)dxdy = \int_{a}^{b} F(x)dx.$$

29

Substituting for $F(x)$ from (9) we see that this equation amounts to the first assertion of (6). The second equality follows from the symmetry in x and y.

Remark. The statement (6) furnishes another proof of the theorem on p. 33 of *IC*, but under somewhat different assumptions.

Example 1. Evaluate

$$I = \iint_Q \frac{dxdy}{x + y + 1}$$

over the square $Q: 0 \leqslant x, y \leqslant 1$. By the preceding theorem

$$I = \int_0^1 dx \int_0^1 \frac{dy}{x + y + 1} = \int_0^1 dx \{\log(x + 2) - \log(x + 1)\}$$
$$= [(x + 2)\log(x + 2) - (x + 2) - (x + 1)\log(x + 1)$$
$$+ x + 1]_0^1 = \log\frac{27}{16}.$$

It is useful to note the following special case. Let $f(x,y) = g(x)h(y)$, where g and h are continuous functions of x and y respectively. If, as before, R denotes the rectangle R: $a \leqslant x \leqslant b, \alpha \leqslant y \leqslant \beta$, we find that

$$\iint_R g(x)h(y)dxdy = \int_a^b dx \int_\alpha^\beta g(x)h(y)dy = \int_b^a g(x)dx \int_\alpha^\beta h(y)dy,$$
$$\iint_R g(x)h(y)dxdy = \left(\int_a^b g(x)dx\right)\left(\int_\alpha^\beta h(y)dy\right). \quad (14)$$

Thus, if the variables in the integrand are separated in this manner the double integral over a rectangle at once reduces to a product of two ordinary integrals. It is important to bear in mind that this simple rule does not in general hold for non-rectangular regions of integration.

Example 2.

$$\iint_R x^2y \; dxdy = \int_a^b x^2 dx \int_\alpha^\beta y \; dy = \tfrac{1}{6}(b^3 - a^3)(\beta^2 - \alpha^2).$$

3. DOUBLE INTEGRALS OVER NORMAL REGIONS

Let D be a normal region relative to the x-axis, given by

$$D: a \leqslant x \leqslant b, \; \phi(x) \leqslant y \leqslant \psi(x), \tag{15}$$

where ϕ and ψ are continuous functions of x, and let $f(x,y)$ be a continuous function in D. We wish to evaluate $\iint_D f(x,y)dxdy$.

The problem is reduced to that of evaluating an integral over a rectangle by adopting the following device. Enclose D in a rectangle $R: a \leqslant x \leqslant b, \; \alpha \leqslant y \leqslant \beta$ (Fig. 14) and define the

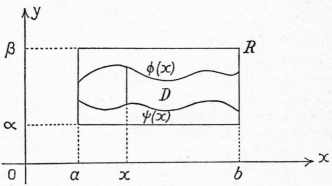

Figure 14.

function f_D throughout R by the rule

$$f_D(x,y) = \begin{cases} f(x,y) \text{ if } (x,y) \in D \\ \quad 0 \;\; \text{ if } (x,y) \notin D, \end{cases} \tag{16}$$

31

DOUBLE INTEGRALS

where the symbol $\in$ means 'belongs to' and $\notin$ its negation. The function f_D is, in general, discontinuous on the arcs $y = \phi(x)$ and $y = \psi(x)$. This does not invalidate the existence of the double integral of f_D over R, and it is clear that

$$\iint_R f_D \, dx \, dy = \iint_D f \, dx \, dy, \tag{17}$$

because the values of f_D outside D make no contribution. But a difficulty arises when we try to invoke Theorem 1 to reduce the integral on the left to a repeated integral. For we have proved this theorem on the assumption that the integrand is continuous throughout R. This step requires further justification, which is outlined in the Appendix (p. 99). Assuming, in the meantime, that the application of Theorem 1 is legitimate, we have that

$$\iint_D f(x,y) \, dx \, dy = \int_a^b dx \int_\alpha^\beta f_D(x,y) \, dy. \tag{18}$$

When x has a fixed value,

$$\int_\alpha^\beta f_D(x,y) \, dy = \int_{\psi(x)}^{\phi(x)} f(x,y) \, dy.$$

For, when we are integrating on the vertical line through the point $(x,0)$ the function f_D is zero above the arc $y = \phi(x)$ and below the arc $y = \psi(x)$, and it is identical with f between those arcs. Substituting in (18) we obtain the required reduction formula, namely

$$\iint_D f(x,y) \, dx \, dy = \int_a^b dx \int_{\psi(x)}^{\phi(x)} f(x,y) \, dy. \tag{19}$$

Similarly, when D is a normal with respect to the y-axis and is defined by

$$D: \alpha \leqslant y \leqslant \beta, \ p(y) \leqslant x \leqslant q(y),$$

32

(see Fig. 9, p. 14) then

$$\iint_D f(x,y)dxdy = \int_\alpha^\beta dy \int_{p(y)}^{q(y)} f(x,y)dx. \qquad (20)$$

The reader should carefully note the general procedure for evaluating a double integral over a normal region D. For example, if D is normal relative to the x-axis, the first step is to ascertain the total variation of x when D is swept out, say $a \leqslant x \leqslant b$. This gives the (constant) limits for the 'outer' integral on the right of (19). Next, consider the variation of y for an arbitrary value of x in the interval $[a,b]$, in other words consider the vertical segment, with abscissa x, lying in D. This segment is given by the inequalities $\psi(x) \leqslant y \leqslant \phi(x)$, which determine the limits for the 'inner' integral. Thus for a non-rectangular region one or both of these limits are not constant. In all cases, it is desirable to sketch the region.

Example 3. Evaluate $\iint_D xy\, dxdy$, where D is the positive quadrant of the unit circle (Fig. 15).

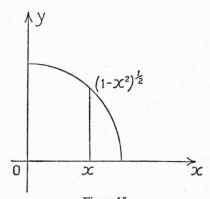

Figure 15.

33

DOUBLE INTEGRALS

This region is normal with respect to both axes. We use formula (19). Thus

$$\iint_D xy\,dxdy = \int_0^1 dx \int_0^{\sqrt{(1-x^2)}} xy\,dy = \int_0^1 x\left[\tfrac{1}{2}y^2\right]_0^{\sqrt{(1-x^2)}} dx$$

$$= \tfrac{1}{2}\int_0^1 x(1-x^2)dx = \tfrac{1}{8}.$$

Example 4. Evaluate $\iint_D (x^2 - y^2)dxdy$, where D is the triangle with vertices $(-1,1)$, $(0,0)$, $(1,1)$. In this example, it is convenient to use the fact that D is normal with respect to the y-axis. Thus, y varies from 0 to 1, and, for a fixed value of y, x ranges from $-y$ to y. Hence, by (19),

$$\int_0^1 dy \int_{-y}^y (x^2 - y^2)dx = \int_0^1 \left[\tfrac{1}{3}x^3 - xy^2\right]_{-y}^y dy$$

$$= \int_0^1 (\tfrac{2}{3}y^3 - 2y^3)dy = -\tfrac{1}{3}.$$

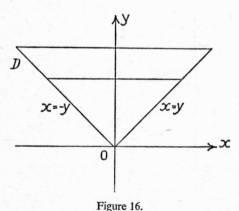

Figure 16.

34

Example 5. Change the order of integration in the repeated integral

$$I = \int_0^a dx \int_0^{a-\sqrt{(a^2-x^2)}} x(y-a)^{-2} \log (y+a) dy \qquad (a > 0)$$

and find its value.

In order to sketch the region (Fig. 17) of the corresponding double integral we observe that the arc

$$y = a - \sqrt{(a^2 - x^2)} \qquad (0 \leqslant x \leqslant a) \qquad (21)$$

is part of the circle $x^2 + (y-a)^2 = a^2$. Since the region is

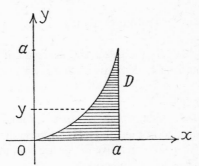

Figure 17.

normal relative to the y-axis, we may apply (20). We shall accordingly write the equation of this arc in the form $x = \sqrt{(2ay - y^2)} = p(y) \ (0 \leqslant y \leqslant a)$. Also $q(y) = a$. Hence

$$I = \int_0^a dy \int_{\sqrt{(2ay-y^2)}}^a x(y-a)^{-2} \log (y+a) dx$$

$$= \int_0^a dy(y-a)^{-2} \log (y+a) \int_{\sqrt{(2ay-y^2)}}^a x \, dx$$

$$= \int_0^a dy(y-a)^{-2} \log (y+a) \left[\tfrac{1}{2}x^2 \right]_{\sqrt{(2ay-y^2)}}^a$$

$$= \tfrac{1}{2} \int_0^a dy(y-a)^{-2} \log (y+a)(a^2 - 2ay + y^2)$$

$$= \tfrac{1}{2} \int_0^a \log (y+a) dy$$

$$= \tfrac{1}{2}a(-1 + \log 4a).$$

4. GREEN'S THEOREM IN TWO DIMENSIONS

It may be asked whether there exists a two-dimensional analogue of the formula

$$\int_a^b f'(x)dx = f(b) - f(a).$$

In other words, do we get a simple result if we form the double integral of a derivative? Since we are dealing with functions of two variables, we shall, of course, have to consider partial derivatives.

Let D be a region which is normal with respect to the x-axis, as indicated in Fig. 14, p. 31. Suppose that the function $P(x,y)$ and its partial derivative $\partial P/\partial y$ are continuous in D and apply (19) to the double integral $\partial P/\partial y$. Thus

$$\iint_D \frac{\partial P}{\partial y} dx dy = \int_a^b dx \int_\psi^\phi \frac{\partial P}{\partial y} dy$$

$$= \int_a^b \{P(x,\phi(x)) - P(x, \psi(x))\} dx.$$

Now the integral on the right is an ordinary integral with respect to x, but the result becomes more interesting if we express it as a line integral over the contour Γ of D. The work is similar to our discussion of area in § 3 of Chapter I. As always, Γ is described in the counter-clockwise sense. We then find that

$$\int_{\Gamma} P \, dx = \int_{a}^{b} P(x,\psi(x))dx + \int_{b}^{a} P(x,\phi(x))dx$$
$$= \int_{a}^{b} \{P(x,\psi(x)) - P(x,\phi(x))\}dx,$$

bearing in mind that the line integrals over the vertical sections $A'A$ and BB' are zero because $dx = 0$ on them. Hence we have proved that

$$\iint_{D} \frac{\partial P}{\partial y}dxdy = - \int_{\Gamma} P \, dx.$$

This is the simplest form of Green's Theorem, valid for regions which are normal relative to the x-axis.

Next, consider a region which is normal relative to the y-axis, see Fig. 9, p. 14. Suppose that $Q(x,y)$ and $\partial Q/\partial x$ are continuous in D. Then

$$\iint_{D} \frac{\partial Q}{\partial x}dxdy = \int_{\alpha}^{\beta} dy \int_{g_2(y)}^{g_1(y)} \frac{\partial Q}{\partial x} \, dx$$
$$= \int_{\alpha}^{\beta} \{Q(g_1(y), y) - Q(g_2(y),y)\}dy.$$

Having regard to our convention about orientation and the fact that $dy = 0$ on the horizontal segments KK' and $L'L$ we find that

$$\int_{\Gamma} Q \, dy = \int_{\alpha}^{\beta} \{Q(g_1(y),y) - Q(g_2(y),y)\}dy.$$

Hence in this case

$$\iint_{D} \frac{\partial Q}{\partial x}dxdy = \int_{\Gamma} Q \, dy.$$

For a region which is normal with respect to both axes we can combine the two results and obtain the important

Theorem 2 (Green's Theorem). Let D be a normal region

bounded by Γ and suppose that P, Q, $\partial P/\partial y$ and $\partial Q/\partial x$ are continuous in D. Then

$$\int_\Gamma P\,dx + Q\,dy = \iint_D \left(\frac{\partial Q}{\partial x} - \frac{\partial P}{\partial y}\right)dxdy. \qquad (22)$$

Example 6. On taking $Q = x$ and $P = -y$ we find that

$$\int_\Gamma x\,dx - y\,dy = \iint_D 2\,dxdy = 2|D|,$$

where $|D|$ is the area of D, see (i) on p. 24. This confirms I, (13) (p. 16) for normal regions.

Example 7. Evaluate $I = \displaystyle\int_\Gamma x^2y^3dx + 3x^3y^2dy$, where Γ is the boundary of the square $D: -1 \leqslant x, y \leqslant 1$. By (22),

$$I = \iint_D \left\{\frac{\partial}{\partial x}(3x^3y^2) - \frac{\partial}{\partial y}(x^2y^3)\right\}dxdy = 6\iint_D x^2y^2dxdy$$

$$= 6\int_{-1}^1 x^2dx\int_{-1}^1 y^2dy = \frac{8}{3}.$$

An interesting situation arises when the functions P and Q satisfy the equation

$$\frac{\partial P}{\partial y} = \frac{\partial Q}{\partial x} \qquad (23)$$

for all points (x,y) in D. Then the integral on the right of (22) is zero and hence

$$\int_\Gamma P\,dx + Q\,dy = 0.$$

We have already seen in I, (7) (p. 10) that (24) holds when

$$P = f_x, \quad Q = f_y, \qquad (24)$$

where f is an arbitrary function satisfying appropriate differentiability conditions. Clearly (23) is a consequence of (24). The converse statement is also true if we make the additional assumption that D is *simply connected*. This means that every loop lying in D encloses a region which is a subset of D; in other words D has no 'holes'. We shall show that in these circumstances (24) holds for any loop in D, that is, we shall construct a function f which satisfies (24). To this end we choose a fixed point (x_0, y_0) and let (x, y) be an arbitrary point

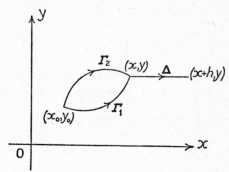

Figure 18.

in D. Let Γ_1 be a path in D which joins the points (x_0, y_0) and (x, y). We assert that the line integral $\displaystyle\int_{\Gamma_1} P\, dx + Q\, dy$ depends only on (x, y), but not on Γ_1. For if Γ_2 is another path in D joining (x_0, y_0) and (x, y), then $\Gamma_0 = \Gamma_1 - \Gamma_2$ is a closed path, where $-\Gamma_2$ denotes the path described in the opposite sense to Γ_2. Hence

$$\int_{\Gamma_1} P\, dx + Q\, dy = 0, \text{ that is } \int_{\Gamma_1} P\, dx + Q\, dy = \int_{\Gamma_2} P\, dx + Q\, dy.$$

We have therefore shown that

$$f(x, y) = \int_{\Gamma_1} P\, dx + Q\, dy \qquad (25)$$

39

is a single-valued function of the coordinates (x,y), since the choice of Γ_1 is immaterial. (The dependence on (x_0,y_0) is ignored.) It remains to verify (24). Thus we have to compute the partial derivatives of f. If Δ is the straight segment joining (x,y) and $(x+h,y)$, we have that

$$f(x+h,y) = \int_{\Gamma_1+\Delta} P\,dx + Q\,dy,$$

and hence

$$f(x+h,y) - f(x,y) = \int_\Delta P\,dx + Q\,dy = \int_\Delta P\,dx,$$

because $dy = 0$ on Δ. Writing the last integral as an ordinary integral with respect to the parameter t we find that

$$\int_\Delta P\,dx = \int_x^{x+h} P(t,y)dt = hP(\xi,y),$$

where ξ is a certain number between x and $x+h$. Hence

$$\frac{f(x+h,y) - f(x,y)}{h} = P(\xi,y).$$

As h tends to zero, we obtain that $f_x(x,y) = P(x,y)$. In the same way it can be shown that $f_y(x,y) = Q(x,y)$.

Finally, we mention an alternative form of Green's Theorem, which is convenient for some applications in Physics. Let* $\mathbf{n} = (n_1,n_2)$ be the unit vector in the direction of the outward drawn normal at an arbitrary point of Γ. If $\mathbf{n}$ makes an angle ϕ with the positive x-direction, $\mathbf{n} = (n_1,n_2) = (\cos\phi, \sin\phi)$. The unit tangent vector is then $(-\sin\phi, \cos\phi)$. On the other hand, if s is chosen as parameter on Γ, the unit tangent vector is $\left(\dfrac{dx}{ds}, \dfrac{dy}{ds}\right)$. Hence $dx/ds = -n_2$, $dy/ds = n_1$. Green's

* K. L. Wardle, loc. cit., Chapter I.

Theorem now becomes

$$\int_{\Gamma}(-n_2 P + n_1 Q)ds = \int\int_D \left(\frac{\partial Q}{\partial x} - \frac{\partial P}{\partial y}\right)dxdy,$$

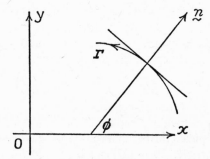

Figure 19.

but it is preferable to write this in a more symmetrical form by putting $Q = P_1$ and $P = -P_2$, where P_1 and P_2 are arbitrary functions of x and y. Thus

$$\int_{\Gamma}(P_1 n_1 + P_2 n_2)ds = \int\int_D \left(\frac{\partial P_1}{\partial x} + \frac{\partial P_2}{\partial y}\right)dxdy. \qquad (26)$$

5. CHANGE OF VARIABLES

Up to now we have given preference to Cartesian coordinates. The configurations of points, curves and regions, which we have so far considered, were assumed to be embedded in a plane, and the coordinates had the usual meaning with reference to a pair of fixed perpendicular axes. Only in I, § 3 did we briefly discuss the effect of rotating the axes and the transition to polar coordinates. It will now be necessary to treat this topic in more detail.

41

Generally, a transformation of variables is given by a pair, μ, of equations

$$\mu: x = p(u,v), \ y = q(u,v), \tag{27}$$

where (u,v) are the 'new' coordinates of the point (x,y). It is convenient to think of (u,v) as a point in the (u,v)-plane, which we consider side by side with the (x,y)-plane. We shall always assume that the functions p and q are continuous and differentiable* in a certain region, E_0, of the (u,v)-plane, and we may describe μ as a *mapping* of E_0 on to a region D_0 of the (x,y)-plane which will be called the image of E_0 under μ. In a brief notation: $D_0 = \mu E_0$. In principle, μ translates all the features of E_0 into corresponding features of D_0. For our purpose it is essential to stipulate further that the mapping is one-to-one and therefore invertible. Thus (27) can be solved for u and v in terms of x and y, giving the inverse mapping

$$\mu^{-1}: u = \phi(x,y), \ v = \psi(x,y) \tag{28}$$

from D_0 on to E_0. The pairs of equations (27) and (28) are in every respect equivalent and contain the same information about D_0 and E_0, like the two parts 'English–French' and 'French–English' of a competent dictionary. For example, subregions, curves and points of D_0 correspond to subregions, curves and points of E_0, and conversely.

We recall† that the condition for the invertibility of μ is that the Jacobian

$$J = \frac{\partial(x,y)}{\partial(u,v)} = \begin{vmatrix} \dfrac{\partial x}{\partial u} & \dfrac{\partial x}{\partial v} \\[2ex] \dfrac{\partial y}{\partial u} & \dfrac{\partial y}{\partial v} \end{vmatrix} \tag{29}$$

* P. J. Hilton, *Partial Derivatives*, in this series, p. 10.
† P. J. Hilton, loc. cit., Theorem 3.2, p. 31.

should be non-zero in E_0. Thus the Jacobian is either always positive or always negative in E_0. There is no loss of generality if we henceforth assume that

$$J > 0; \tag{30}$$

for if not, we need only interchange the roles of u and v, which has the effect of multiplying J by -1.

We remind the reader of the multiplication formula*

$$\frac{\partial(x,y)}{\partial(\xi,\eta)} = \frac{\partial(x,y)}{\partial(u,v)} \frac{\partial(u,v)}{\partial(\xi,\eta)} \tag{31}$$

and of the fact that the Jacobian of the inverse mapping is J^{-1}, that is

$$\frac{\partial(u,v)}{\partial(x,y)} = 1 \Big/ \frac{\partial(x,y)}{\partial(u,v)}. \tag{32}$$

Example 8. A linear mapping is given by equations of the form

$$x = a_1u + b_1v + c_1, \; y = a_2u + b_2v + c_2, \tag{33}$$

where a_i, b_i, c_i ($i = 1,2$) are constants such that

$$J = a_1b_2 - a_2b_1 > 0. \tag{34}$$

It is known from elementary algebra that this condition ensures the invertibility of (33). In this case E_0 and D_0 may be taken to be the entire planes.

Example 9. The transformation to polar coordinates is represented by the equations

$$x = r \cos \theta, \; y = r \sin \theta, \tag{35}$$

where we have used the traditional notation (r, θ) rather than (u, v).

---

* P. J. Hilton, loc. cit., p. 35.

DOUBLE INTEGRALS

In this case

$$J = \begin{vmatrix} \dfrac{\partial x}{\partial r} & \dfrac{\partial x}{\partial \theta} \\[2ex] \dfrac{\partial y}{\partial r} & \dfrac{\partial y}{\partial \theta} \end{vmatrix} = \begin{vmatrix} \cos\theta & -r\sin\theta \\[1ex] \sin\theta & r\cos\theta \end{vmatrix} = r, \qquad (36)$$

which happens to be independent of θ. But $J = 0$ when $r = 0$, and we must therefore restrict the mapping to regions which do not contain the origin; also the nature of the variables is such that $r < 0$ makes no sense. It is instructive to consider the mapping (35) in more detail. The image of the rectangle

$$E: 0 < a \leqslant r \leqslant 1, \quad 0 \leqslant \theta \leqslant 2\pi$$

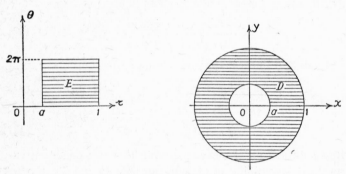

Figure 20.

is the annulus bounded by the circles $x^2 + y^2 = a^2$ and $x^2 + y^2 = 1$. If we had taken $a = 0$, the image would have been the whole of the unit disc, but the mapping would no longer have been one-to-one, as the whole of the segment $r = 0$, $0 \leqslant \theta \leqslant 2\pi$ would have been mapped into the point $x = y = 0$.

Returning to the general case, consider a loop, Δ, in E_0 bounding a region E and let Γ and D be the images of Δ and E

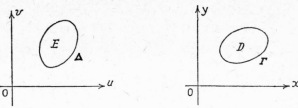

Figure 21.

under the mapping μ. We wish to express the area of D in terms of u and v. In order to avoid analytical complications we shall here assume that the transformation functions p and q have partial derivatives up to the second order, and we shall further suppose that D and E are normal regions. Let

$$\Delta: u = \phi(t), \, v = \psi(t) \qquad (\alpha \leqslant t \leqslant \beta)$$

be a set of parametric equations for Δ. This induces a parametric equation for Γ, namely

$$\Gamma: x = p(\phi(t), \psi(t)), \, y = q(\phi(t), \psi(t)) \qquad (\alpha \leqslant t \leqslant \beta).$$

Using the formula I, (12) for the area of D we have that

$$|D| = \int_{\Gamma} x \, dy = \int_{\alpha}^{\beta} x\dot{y} \, dt,$$

where the dot denotes differentiation with respect to t. By the formula* for differentiating composite functions, $\dot{y} = y_u \dot{u} + y_v \dot{v}$, whence

$$|D| = \int_{\alpha}^{\beta} (xy_u\dot{u} + xy_v\dot{v})dt.$$

This integral may be interpreted as a line integral over Δ, in fact

$$|D| = \int_{\Delta} xy_u du + xy_v dv,$$

* P. J. Hilton, loc. cit., equation (26), p. 13.

45

where all functions are supposed to be expressed in terms of u and v. From now we shall operate in the (u,v)-plane. Applying Green's Theorem to the last integral we find that

$$|D| = \int\int_E \left\{ \frac{\partial}{\partial u}(xy_v) - \frac{\partial}{\partial v}(xy_u) \right\} du dv$$

$$= \int\int_E (x_u y_v + xy_{uv} - x_v y_u - xy_{uv}) du dv$$

$$= \int\int_E (x_u y_v - x_v y_u) du dv.$$

We have therefore established the important result that

$$|D| = \int\int_E J(u,v) du dv. \tag{37}$$

Notice that the second derivatives, whose existence we had postulated, only made a transitory appearance.

The assumption that D and E are normal regions is somewhat restrictive, but most regions which occur in practice, are either normal or can be regarded as the union of finitely many normal regions.

We mention a consequence of (37) which will be of interest later, when we shall apply this result to 'small' regions. Since the first order derivatives of p and q are continuous in E_0, the function J is continuous in E. Hence by the Mean Value Theorem, there exists at least one point (u_0,v_0) in E such that

$$|D| = J(u_0,v_0)|E|. \tag{38}$$

There is an alternative way of interpreting the transformation (27), which affords a more intuitive understanding of its significance. According to this view we consider only one plane, the original (x,y)-plane, and we use the two equations of (27) to define two families of curves. Thus if $u = u_1$ is constant, the equations $x = p(u_1,v)$, $y = q(u_1,v)$ can be re-

garded as parametric equations of a curve in the (x,y)-plane
with parameter v; this curve will simply be called 'the curve u_1',
and we get a family of curves by letting u take different constant values u_1, u_2, u_3, ... Now two members of this family
cannot intersect in virtue of the one-to-one property of the
transformation, for this would mean that for certain values
u_1, u_2, v_1, v_2, $p(u_1,v_1) = p(u_2,v_2)$ and $q(u_1,v_1) = q(u_2,v_2)$. Similarly,
we obtain a second family of curves by taking v to be constant
and regarding u as a parameter. A typical member of this

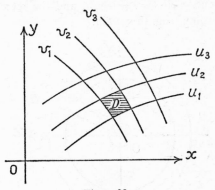

Figure 22.

family, where $v = const$, is given by the equations $x = p(u,v_1)$,
$y = q(u,v_1)$. Every member of the family $u = const$ meets
every member of the family $v = const$ at exactly one point.
For example the curves $u = u_1$ and $v = v_1$ meet at (u_1,v_1). The
situation is analogous to the way in which the points on the
surface of the earth, other than the poles, are specified by the
circles of longitude and latitude which form two families of
curves.

Let us now select two members from each of the two fami-
lies, say $u = u_1$, $u = u_2$, $v = v_1$ and $v = v_2$, where $u_1 < u_2$ and

$v_1 < v_2$. These four curves bound a region, D, in the (x,y)-plane, which is the image of the rectangle

$$E: u_1 \leqslant u \leqslant u_2, v_1 \leqslant v \leqslant v_2$$

in the (u,v)-plane. Hence, by (37),

$$|D| = \int\int_E J(u,v)dudv = J(u_0,v_0)(u_2 - u_1)(v_2 - v_1), \quad (39)$$

where (u_0,v_0) is suitable point in D.

In the case of polar coordinates the two families are the set of concentric circles $r = const$, and the set of half-lines $\theta = const$ issuing from the origin.

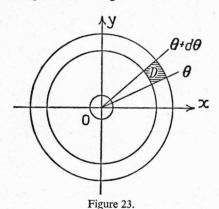

Figure 23.

Example 9. Find the area, in the positive quadrant, bounded by the curves $xy = a$, $xy = b$, $y^2 = \alpha x$, $y^2 = \beta x$, where $0 < a < b$ and $0 < \alpha < \beta$.

Put $u = xy$, $v = y^2/x$. The region D is the image of the rectangle $E: a \leqslant u \leqslant b, \alpha \leqslant v \leqslant \beta$ in the (u,v)-plane. In order to find the Jacobian $\dfrac{\partial(x,y)}{\partial(u,v)}$ it is slightly more convenient to obtain

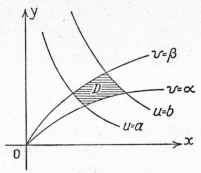

Figure 24.

first its reciprocal

$$\frac{\partial(u,v)}{\partial(x,y)} = \begin{vmatrix} y & x \\ -\dfrac{y^2}{x^2} & \dfrac{2y}{x} \end{vmatrix} = \frac{3y^2}{x} = 3v.$$

Hence $J = 1/3v$, which is indeed positive in the region E. By (37),

$$|D| = \tfrac{1}{3}\iint_E v^{-1}dudv = \tfrac{1}{3}\int_a^b du \int_\alpha^\beta v^{-1}\,dv = \tfrac{1}{3}(b-a)\log(\beta/\alpha).$$

6. TRANSFORMATION OF DOUBLE INTEGRALS

One of the most powerful tools for evaluating a double integral is to change the variables of integration in order to reduce it to an integral that is easier to handle. This is analogous to the 'method of substitution' used for ordinary integrals. We recall that even in this elementary case the procedure involves three distinct steps. If in the integral $\int_a^b f(x)dx$ we wish to introduce a new variable of integration by the invertible substitution

49

$x = p(u)$, we have (i) to express the integrand in terms of u, thus $f(x) = f(p(u)) = g(u)$ say, (ii) change the limits of integration to α, β where $a = p(\alpha)$, $b = p(\beta)$ and (iii) replace the 'differential' dx by $p'(u)du$. We shall see that these three features will appear again when we transform the double integral

$$\iint_D f(x,y)dxdy \qquad (40)$$

by introducing new variables u,v. Using the same notation as in the preceding section we employ an invertible mapping

$$\mu: x = p(u,v),\ y = q(u,v)$$
$$\mu^{-1}: u = P(x,y),\ v = Q(x,y)$$

and we suppose that D is the image of E; in symbols $D = \mu E$ or, equivalently, $E = \mu^{-1}D$. Going back to first principles, we choose a subdivision Δ of D, thus

$$\Delta:\ \sigma_1,\ \sigma_2,\ \ldots,\ \sigma_n.$$

Under μ^{-1}, this corresponds to a subdivision of E which we may denote by $\mu^{-1}\Delta$, say

$$\mu^{-1}\Delta:\ \tau_1,\ \tau_2,\ \ldots,\ \tau_n.$$

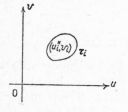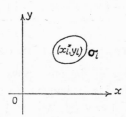

Figure 25.

By (39), there exists a point (u_i,v_i) in τ_i such that

$$|\sigma_i| = J(u_i,v_i)|\tau_i|.$$

Let (x_i,y_i) be the image of (u_i,v_i) under μ, that is $x_i = p(u_i,v_i)$,

$y_i = q(u_i,v_i)$. Then (x_i,y_i) is a point of σ_i. We choose this point for $i = 1, 2, \ldots, n$ to form the approximation sum

$$S(\Delta) = \sum_{i=1}^{n} f(x_i,y_i)|\sigma_i|,$$

which, as we know, tends to (40) as Δ runs through a sequence of subdivisions whose norms tend to zero. Expressing f in terms of u and v we shall write

$$f(x,y) = f(p(u,v), q(u,v)) = g(u,v) \qquad (41)$$

and hence

$$f(x_i,y_i) = g(u_i,v_i).$$

Thus on substituting for $|\sigma_i|$ we find that

$$S(\Delta) = \sum_{i=1}^{n} g(u_i,v_i)\, J(u_i,v_i)|\tau_i|.$$

Now this is an approximation sum for an integral over E, the integrand being $g(u,v)J(u,v)$. For it can be shown* that, as the norm of Δ tends to zero, the norm of $\mu^{-1}\Delta$ will likewise tend to zero. Thus the limit of $S(\Delta)$ appears under two forms and on equating them we obtain the desired result, namely

$$\iint_D f(x,y)dxdy = \iint_E g(u,v)\, J(u,v)dudv, \qquad (42)$$

where g is defined in (41). We repeat that our transformations are restricted by the condition that $J(u,v) > 0$ in E. If we demand only that $J(u,v) \neq 0$, then in the last integral J has to be replaced by $|J|$. Summing up we observe that changing the variables of integration in a double integral involves three steps, namely (i) *introducing a pair of new variables u, v by an invertible mapping and expressing the integrand in terms of these new variables;* (ii) *changing the region of integration;* (iii) *replacing dxdy by J(u,v)dudv.* The intuitive meaning of the last

* Theorem on uniform continuity, see R. Courant, loc. cit., p. 97.

step is best understood by referring to Fig. 22 and formula (39) of p. 48. If we put $u_1 = u$, $u_2 = u + du$, $v_1 = v$, $v_2 = v + dv$ and ignore the variation of J in the mesh by writing $J(u,v)$ in place of $J(u_0,v_0)$, we find that the area of a typical mesh becomes

$$J(u,v)dudv.$$

This expression is often called the *element of area* in the (u,v)-system of coordinates.

For the original Cartesian coordinates we have, of course, that $J(x,y) = \partial(x,y)/\partial(x,y) = 1$. The network then consists of straight lines parallel to the coordinate axes so that the element of area is $dxdy$, which explains the occurrence of this symbol in the original notation for the double integral. The value of the element of area can often be guessed by inspecting the curvilinear network and using geometrical arguments to obtain the area of a typical mesh. Thus in Fig. 23 the shaded region is bounded by the curves which are specified by the values r, $r + dr$, θ and $\theta + d\theta$ in their respective families, and the area of this region is $\frac{1}{2}(r + dr)^2 d\theta - \frac{1}{2}r^2 d\theta$, which, to a first approximation, becomes $rdrd\theta$. This agrees with $J(r,\theta)drd\theta$, since, by (36), $J(r,\theta) = r$.

Finally, we remark that (42) is a generalization of (37), to which it reduces when $f = 1$.

Example 10. Evaluate $\iint_D xy\, dxdy$, where D is the positive quadrant of the disc $x^2 + y^2 \leqslant a^2$.

If we change to polar coordinates, the disc is the image of the rectangle E: $0 \leqslant r \leqslant a$, $0 \leqslant \theta \leqslant \dfrac{\pi}{2}$ in the (r,θ) plane. However, a difficulty arises because the Jacobian, $J = r$, vanishes at the origin. We must therefore cut out a small region C_ρ from D,

52

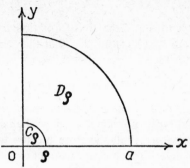

Figure 26.

which is the intersection of D with the disc $x^2 + y^2 \leqslant \rho^2$.
Let $D_\rho = D - C_\rho$. Then, clearly,

$$\iint_D xy\, dxdy = \iint_{D_\rho} xy\, dxdy + \iint_{C_\rho} xy\, dxdy.$$

If (x,y) lies in C_ρ, $|x| \leqslant \rho$ and $|y| \leqslant \rho$. Also $|C_\rho| = \frac{1}{4}\pi\rho^2$.
Hence

$$\left| \iint_D xy\, dxdy - \iint_{D_\rho} xy\, dxdy \right| = \left| \iint_{C_\rho} xy\, dxdy \right| \leqslant \frac{1}{4}\pi\rho^4.$$

It follows that $\displaystyle\iint_D xy\, dxdy = \lim_{\rho \to 0} \iint_{D_\rho} xy\, dxdy$.

Now D_ρ is the image of the rectangle E_ρ: $\rho \leqslant r \leqslant a$,
$0 \leqslant \theta \leqslant \frac{1}{2}\pi$ and J is positive in E_ρ. Therefore

$$\iint_{D_\rho} xy\, dxdy = \iint_{E_\rho} r^2 \cos\theta \sin\theta\, r\, drd\theta$$

$$= \int_\rho^a r^3 dr \int_0^{\pi/2} \cos\theta \sin\theta\, d\theta = \tfrac{1}{8}(a^4 - \rho^4).$$

On letting ρ tend to zero, we find that

$$\iint_D xy\, dxdy = \tfrac{1}{8}a^4.$$

53

We should have arrived at the same result if we had been careless enough to apply the transformation formula to the whole disc despite the fact that $J = 0$ at the origin. However, the foregoing argument shows that this error is harmless, and the same consideration applies to any integral $\iint_D f\,dxdy$, in which the integrand remains bounded at the origin and, indeed, to more general types of integrand, as we shall see in the next section. In future, we shall therefore use the transformation to polar coordinates in such cases, without explicitly repeating the above limit process.

Example 11. Evaluate $I = \iint_D \{a^2 + (x - y)^2\}^{-\frac{1}{2}}dxdy$, where D is the square $D: 0 \leqslant x \leqslant a, 0 \leqslant y \leqslant a$. Change the variables to $u = x - y$, $v = y$ or conversely, put $x = u + v$, $y = v$. The Jacobian is equal to the determinant of this linear transformation and hence equal to 1. The region E, which corresponds to D, is the parallelogram

$$E: 0 \leqslant u + v \leqslant a, \quad 0 \leqslant v \leqslant a \qquad \text{(see Fig. 27)}$$

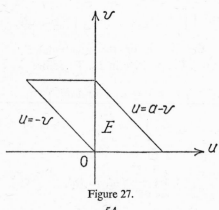

Figure 27.

54

Hence $I = \displaystyle\int_0^a dv \int_{-v}^{a-v} \{a^2 + u^2\}^{-\frac{1}{2}} du$

$$= \int_0^a \left\{ \sinh^{-1} \frac{a-v}{a} + \sinh^{-1} \frac{v}{a} \right\} dv.$$

On putting $v = at$ we find that

$$I = a \int_0^1 \{\sinh^{-1}(1-t) + \sinh^{-1}t\} dt = 2a \int_0^1 \sinh^{-1}t\, dt,$$

having replaced t by $1 - t$ in the first term. Integration by parts yields

$$I = 2a[t \sinh^{-1}t - (1 + t^2)^{\frac{1}{2}}]_0^1 = 2a(\sinh^{-1}1 + 1 - \sqrt{2}),$$
$$I = 2a\{\log(1 + \sqrt{2}) + 1 - \sqrt{2}\}.$$

Example 12. If D is the triangle $D: x \geqslant 0,\ y \geqslant 0,\ x + y \leqslant 1$ and $f(t)$ any function which is continuous for $0 \leqslant t \leqslant 1$, then

$$\iint_D f(x+y)x^\alpha y^\beta dx\, dy = \frac{\alpha!\beta!}{(\alpha+\beta+1)!} \int_0^1 f(t) t^{\alpha+\beta+1} dt. \quad (43)$$

This is known as *Dirichlet's formula* (for two variables.) The formula is valid provided that $\alpha > -1$ and $\beta > -1$, but we

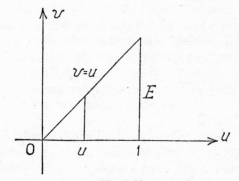

Figure 28.

DOUBLE INTEGRALS

shall prove it in the first instance only on the assumption that $\alpha \geqslant 0, \beta \geqslant 0$ (see p. 60).

We make the substitution $x = u - v$, $y = v$. The Jacobian is equal to 1. The region E is bounded by $u - v \geqslant 0$, $v \geqslant 0$ and $u \leqslant 1$ and is therefore the triangle shown in Fig. 28. Hence the integral on the left of (43) becomes

$$J = \int\int_E f(u)(u-v)^\alpha v^\beta \, du \, dv = \int_0^1 du \, f(u) \int_0^u (u-v)^\alpha v^\beta dv.$$

On putting $v = ut$ in the inner integral we find that

$$J = \int_0^1 du \, f(u) \int_0^1 u^\alpha (1-t)^\alpha u^\beta t^\beta u \, dt,$$

$$J = \int_0^1 du \, f(u) u^{\alpha+\beta+1} \int_0^1 (1-t)^\alpha t^\beta dt.$$

Now the inner integral is independent of u. By *IC*, p. 47, equation (21), its value is $\alpha!\beta!/(\alpha+\beta+1)!$, which establishes the result.

7. IMPROPER INTEGRALS

In the Existence Theorem (p. 23) it was assumed that (i) the integrand f was bounded and that (ii) the region of integration, D, was finite. In certain circumstances the double integral can still be defined by a limiting process although conditions (i) or (ii) or both are no longer satisfied. Such integrals are called improper integrals. The general situation can be very complicated and we have to confine ourselves to a discussion of a few special cases.

(i) *Unbounded integrand.* In practice, this usually means that the function $f(x,y)$ tends to infinity at one or several isolated points or, worse still, along a whole curve. We begin with the simplest case, in which there is only one singular point in D.

56

In order to simplify the notation we assume that this point is the origin. For the moment we shall make the additional assumption that the integrand is never negative in D, and we shall denote it by p rather than f. For every positive number ρ, let $Z_\rho: x^2 + y^2 \leqslant \rho^2$ be the disc of radius ρ with centre O, and let Z'_ρ be its complement in the plane. Put $D_\rho = D \cap Z'_\rho$, that

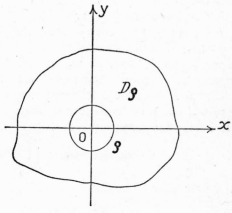

Figure 29.

is D is the region obtained from D by removing Z_ρ or that part of it which lies in D. According to our hypothesis the integral $\iint_{D_\rho} p \, dxdy$ has a finite value for every positive ρ, and it may happen that these values tend to a finite limit as ρ tends to zero. In that case we define

$$\iint_D p \, dxdy = \lim_{\rho \to 0} \iint_{D_\rho} p \, dxdy.$$

It is clear that the integral on the right is a monotone increasing function of ρ. For as ρ tends to zero, the region D_ρ increases

57

and so does the integral because p is non-negative. The existence of the limit is therefore guaranteed if it can be shown that the integral remains bounded as ρ decreases to zero.

We have used a family of discs to cut out the singularity at the origin. Any other family of regions, $\{T_\lambda\}$, for example squares, could have been employed equally well, provided that they contract towards the origin in the following sense: (a) $T_\lambda \subseteq T_\mu$ if $\lambda < \mu$; (b) for every ρ, there exists a λ such that $T_\lambda \subseteq Z_\rho$; (c) for every σ, there exists a μ such that $Z_\sigma \subseteq T_\mu$. We omit the formal proof of this statement.

Many of the questions that arise in connection with improper integrals are analogous to those which concern infinite series. For example, we have the following *comparison test*: let p and q be continuous in D except at 0, where both functions tend to infinity and suppose that $0 \leqslant p(x,y) \leqslant q(x,y)$ in D. Then if $\iint_D q\,dxdy$ exists, the integral $\iint_D p\,dxdy$ also exists and $\iint_D p\,dxdy \leqslant \iint_D q\,dxdy$.

Next we have the proposition that *absolute convergence implies convergence*. Thus if $\iint_D |f|\,dxdy$ exists, then $\iint_D f\,dxdy$ also exists. For $0 \leqslant \frac{1}{2}\{|f|-f\} \leqslant |f|$ and $0 \leqslant \frac{1}{2}\{|f|+f\} \leqslant |f|$, so that the integrals of $\frac{1}{2}\{|f|-f\}$ and $\frac{1}{2}\{|f|+f\}$ exist. Hence the integral of $\frac{1}{2}\{|f|+f\} - \frac{1}{2}\{|f|-f\} = f$ also exists.

The following result is useful in many cases.

Theorem 3. *Let g be continuous in D and suppose that $|g(x,y)| \leqslant M$ in D. Then the integral*

$$\iint_D (x^2 + y^2)^{-\alpha} g(x,y)dxdy$$

exists provided that $\alpha < 1$.

Proof. By the comparison test, it is sufficient to prove that

$\iint_D (x^2 + y^2)^{-\alpha} dxdy$ exists. Let $E: x^2 + y^2 \leqslant 1$ be the unit

disc and write $D = (D \cap E) \cup (D \cap \mathscr{C}E) = D_0 \cup D_1$, say, where $\mathscr{C}E$ denotes the complement of E. There is no difficulty about the integral over D_1, as it avoids the origin. Hence it suffices to prove that the integral over D_0 exists. Again, since $D_0 \subseteq E$ and the integrand is positive, it is enough to show that the integral over E exists, and this we shall now proceed to do.

As required by the definition we cut out the disc Z_ρ from E and obtain the annulus $E_\rho: \rho \leqslant x^2 + y^2 \leqslant 1$. Using polar coordinates we find that

$$\iint_{E_\rho} (x^2 + y^2)^{-\alpha} dxdy = \int_\rho^1 dr \int_0^{2\pi} r^{-2\alpha} r \, drd\theta$$

$$= 2\pi \int_\rho^1 r^{-(2\alpha-1)} dr = \frac{\pi}{1-\alpha}(1 - \rho^{-2\alpha+2}).$$

When $\rho \to 0$, this tends to a finite limit, in fact to $\pi(1 - \alpha)^{-1}$, provided that $\alpha < 1$. This proves the theorem.

So far we have considered functions with only one singularity. When singularities occur along a curve, the definition of the improper integral has to be modified accordingly. For

example, in the double integral $\iint_D x^{-\alpha}y^{-\beta} dxdy$, where

$D: 0 \leqslant x, y \leqslant 1$ and $0 < \alpha < 1, 0 < \beta < 1$, the integrand becomes infinite on each of the coordinate axes. It is then necessary to cut out these singularities by strips parallel to the axes and to reduce the region of integration to

$$D_{\rho,\sigma}: \rho \leqslant x \leqslant 1, \quad \sigma \leqslant y \leqslant 1,$$

where $\rho > 0$ and $\sigma > 0$. Then

$$\iint_{D_{\rho,\sigma}} x^{-\alpha}y^{-\beta}dxdy = (1-\alpha)^{-1}(1-\beta)^{-1}(1-\rho^{1-\alpha})(1-\sigma^{1-\beta})$$

and this tends to a finite limit, namely $(1-\alpha)^{-1}(1-\beta)^{-1}$, as $\rho \to 0$ and $\sigma \to 0$. We shall therefore define

$$\iint_D x^{-\alpha}y^{-\beta}dxdy = \lim_{\rho \to 0, \sigma \to 0} \iint_{D_{\rho,\sigma}} x^{-\alpha}y^{-\beta}dxdy$$
$$= (1-\alpha)^{-1}(1-\beta)^{-1}.$$

By an extension of this argument we can show that the formula (43) is valid when $\alpha > -1$ and $\beta > -1$.

(ii) *Infinite region.* We now assume that D cannot be contained in a finite circle, but that the integral of f exists when the region of integration is any finite part of D.

First suppose that the integrand is a non-negative function p and, as before, put $Z_\rho: x^2 + y^2 \leqslant \rho^2$. Now let $D_\rho = D \cap Z_\rho$. Then by hypothesis $\iint_{D_\rho} p\,dxdy$ has a finite value for each ρ, and we shall define

$$\iint_D p\,dxdy = \lim_{\rho \to \infty} \iint_{D_\rho} p\,dxdy, \qquad (44)$$

provided that this limit exists. The fact that we have cut out finite portions from D by means of discs is not important. We could equally well have taken other families of regions which tend to infinity in all directions, for example the family of squares $T_\lambda: -\lambda \leqslant x, y \leqslant \lambda$, where $\lambda \to \infty$. For since the integrand is non-negative, it can easily be shown that

$$\lim_{\lambda \to \infty} \iint_{T_\lambda} p\,dxdy = \lim_{\rho \to \infty} \iint_{D_\lambda} p\,dxdy$$

in the sense that if one of these limits exists, so does the other and the limits are equal, or else neither limit exists.

As an illustration we consider the integral

$$I = \int\int_R e^{-x^2-y^2}dxdy,$$

where $R: -\infty < x, y < \infty$ is the entire plane. First, we must show that this improper integral exists. In this case $R \cap Z_\rho = Z_\rho$ and we have to examine

$$I_\rho = \int\int_{Z_\rho} e^{-(x^2+y^2)}dxdy.$$

This integral is easily evaluated by using polar coordinates. Since the integrand remains bounded at O, where the Jacobian vanishes, this transformation is legitimate (p. 54). Hence

$$I_\rho = \int_0^{2\pi} d\theta \int_0^\rho e^{-r^2} r\, dr = 2\pi\left[-\tfrac{1}{2}e^{-r^2}\right]_0^\rho = \pi(1 - e^{-\rho^2}).$$

On letting ρ tend to infinity we find that

$$\int\int_R e^{-x^2-y^2}dxdy = \pi.$$

Next, we shall try to evaluate the same integral by employing the family of squares $T_\lambda: -\lambda \leqslant x, y \leqslant \lambda$, where $\lambda \to \infty$. Put

$$J_\lambda = \int\int_{T_\lambda} e^{-x^2-y^2}dxdy = \left(\int_{-\lambda}^\lambda e^{-x^2}dx\right)\left(\int_{-\lambda}^\lambda e^{-y^2}dy\right),$$

$$J_\lambda = 4\left(\int_0^\lambda e^{-x^2}dx\right)^2.$$

From the foregoing calculation we know that $\lim_{\lambda\to\infty} J_\lambda = \pi$. This shows that the ordinary integral on the right converges as $\lambda \to \infty$, and in fact

$$\int_0^\infty e^{-x^2}dx = \tfrac{1}{2}\sqrt{\pi}. \tag{45}$$

This provides an alternative proof of the formula (24) given on p. 50 of *IC* (*Poisson's Integral*).

DOUBLE INTEGRALS

8. VOLUMES

A function $z = \phi(x,y)$ which is continuous in a region D of the (x,y)-plane, defines a surface, S, in three-dimensional space. This surface is the set of points $(x,y, \phi(x,y))$, where $(x,y) \in D$.

Suppose, first, that $\phi \geqslant 0$ in D. Then D and S, together with the vertical lines erected at the boundary points of D, enclose a solid region T. At this stage we assume that we have an intuitive idea of what is meant by volume. In particular, we shall accept the formula '*base* $\times$ *height*' for a right cylinder. Our object is to express the volume, $|T|$, of T in terms of ϕ and D. Make a subdivision Δ: $\sigma_1, \sigma_2, \ldots, \sigma_n$ of D. This leads to a subdivision for T which we indicate by $T = T_1 \cup T_2 \cup \ldots \cup T_n$, where T_i is the portion of T having base σ_i. The top of T_i is that part of S which lies above σ_i. Thus T_i is approximately a thin cylinder, except that its top is not in general horizontal. Now if m_i and M_i are the least and the greatest values of ϕ in σ_i, we can state that T_i is contained between two cylinders, both with base σ_i, and with heights m_i and M_i respectively. Hence

$$m_i|\sigma_i| \leqslant |T_i| \leqslant M_i|\sigma_i| \qquad (i = 1, 2, \ldots, n).$$

Since ϕ is continuous, there exists a point (ξ_i, η_i) in σ_i such that

$$|T_i| = \phi(\xi_i, \eta_i)|\sigma_i|.$$

On summing over i we find that $|T| = \sum_{i=1}^{n} \phi(\xi_i, \eta_i)|\sigma_i|$. This is an approximation sum for the double integral of ϕ over D. Hence by letting Δ run through a set of subdivisions whose norms tend to zero, we obtain that

$$|T| = \int\int_D \phi(x,y)dxdy. \tag{46}$$

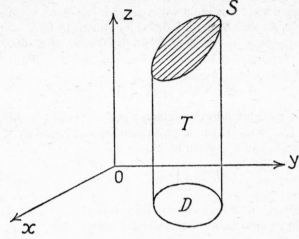

Figure 30.

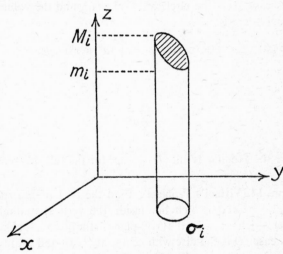

Figure 31.

63

Having derived this result with the aid of our naive notion of volume, we shall henceforth define the volume by (46).

More generally, we shall define the volume of a solid, T, which is *normal with respect to the z-axis*. Such a solid is the set of points (x,y,z) satisfying

$$T: \phi_2(x,y) \leqslant z \leqslant \phi_1(x,y), \quad (x,y) \in D.$$

Thus T is bounded by the surfaces $z = \phi_2(x,y)$ and $z = \phi_1(x,y)$ and by the vertical 'mantle' passing through the boundary of D. The volume of T is given by

$$|T| = \int\int_D (\phi_1 - \phi_2)dxdy. \tag{47}$$

Example 13. Find the volume of the sphere $x^2 + y^2 + z^2 \leqslant a^2$. It is more convenient to consider the hemisphere

$$z = (a^2 - x^2 - y^2)^{\frac{1}{2}} \quad (z > 0).$$

In this case, D is the circle $x^2 + y^2 \leqslant a^2$, and the volume of the hemisphere is

$$\int\int_D (a^2 - x^2 - y^2)^{\frac{1}{2}}dxdy = \int_0^{2\pi} d\theta \int_0^a (a^2 - r^2)^{\frac{1}{2}}r \, dr$$

$$= 2\pi \left[-\frac{1}{3}(a^2 - r^2)^{\frac{3}{2}} \right]_0^a$$

$$= \frac{2\pi}{3}a^3,$$

whence the familiar result $|T| = \dfrac{4\pi}{3}a^3$ for the full sphere.

Example 14 (Viviani's Problem). Find the part of the sphere $x^2 + y^2 + z^2 \leqslant a^2$ which lies inside the vertical (unlimited) cylinder which intersects the (x,y)-plane in the disc $x^2 + y^2 \leqslant ax$. In this case, D is the disc with centre at $(\frac{1}{2}a,0)$ and radius $\frac{1}{2}a$. Introducing polar coordinates, we find that the boundary of D

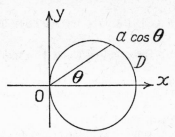

Figure 32.

is given by $r = a \cos \theta$. Thus the limits of integration are not constant, and it is convenient to take the outside integral with respect to θ, where $-\dfrac{\pi}{2} \leqslant \theta \leqslant \dfrac{\pi}{2}$. Since the integrand is $z = (a^2 - x^2 - y)^{\frac{1}{2}}$ $(z \geqslant 0)$, we find that

$$\tfrac{1}{2}|T| = \int_{-\frac{\pi}{2}}^{\frac{\pi}{2}} d\theta \int_0^{a\cos\theta} (a^2 - r^2)^{\frac{1}{2}} r\, dr = \int_{-\frac{\pi}{2}}^{\frac{\pi}{2}} d\theta \left[-\frac{1}{3}(a^2 - r^2)^{\frac{3}{2}} \right]_0^{a\cos\theta}$$

$$= \frac{1}{3}\int_{-\frac{\pi}{2}}^{\frac{\pi}{2}} \{a^3 - a^3 \sin^3\theta\}d\theta = \frac{2a^3}{3} \int_0^{\frac{\pi}{2}} (1 - \sin^3\theta)d\theta$$

$$= \frac{2a^3}{3}\left(\frac{\pi}{2} - \frac{2}{3}\right),$$

whence

$$|T| = \frac{2a^3}{9}(3\pi - 4).$$

DOUBLE INTEGRALS

EXERCISES ON CHAPTER TWO

1. Apply Green's Theorem to evaluate $\int_\Gamma y^2x\,dy - x^2y\,dx$, where

   Γ is the contour consisting of the semicircle $x^2 + y^2 = a^2$ $(y > 0)$ and the segment $(-a,a)$ of the x-axis, described in the counter-clockwise sense. Check your result by evaluating the line integral as it stands.

2. Using the same contour as in the preceding exercise, determine

   a function f such that $\int_\Gamma f(y)dx + x \cos y\,dy = 0$.

3. By changing the order of integration show that
   $$\int_0^{\pi/2} dx \int_x^{\pi/2} \frac{\sin y}{y}dy = 1.$$

4. Show that, as $\delta \to 0$, $\int_0^1 dx \int_\delta^1 \frac{x-y}{(x+y)^3}\,dy \to \tfrac{1}{2}$ and
   $$\int_\delta^1 dy \int_0^1 \frac{x-y}{(x+y)^3}dx \to -\tfrac{1}{2}.$$

   Comment on these results.

5. Show that, if $a > 0$, $\int_0^a dy \int_{y^2/a}^y f(x,y)dx = \int_0^a dx \int_x^{\sqrt{(ax)}} f(x,y)dy$.

   Prove that $\int_0^a y\,dy \int_{y^2/a}^y (a-x)^{-1}(ax - y^2)^{-\frac{1}{2}}dx = \tfrac{1}{2}\pi a$.

6. Evaluate $\iint_D (a^2 - x^2 - y^2)^{\frac{1}{3}}dxdy$, where D is the disc
   $$x^2 + y^2 - ax \leqslant 0.$$

7. Evaluate $\iint_D \exp(ax + by)dxdy$, where D is the triangle bounded by the lines $x = 0$, $y = 0$ and $ax + by = 1$ $(a > 0, b > 0)$.

8. Evaluate $\iint_D (x^4 - y^4)dxdy$, where D is the part of the positive quadrant in which $1 \leqslant x^2 - y^2 \leqslant 2$, $1 \leqslant xy \leqslant 2$.

EXERCISES

9. Find the area bounded by the curves $x^2 + 2y^2 = 1$, $x^2 + 2y^2 = 2$, $2y = x$, $y = 2x$.

10. Prove that if $0 < \alpha < \pi$,

$$\iint_Q \exp(-x^2 - 2xy \cos \alpha - y^2) dx dy = \tfrac{1}{2}\alpha/\sin \alpha,$$

where Q is the positive quadrant of the (x,y)-plane.

11. Evaluate $\iint x^2 y^2 (y^2 - x^2) dx dy$ over the region in the first quadrant bounded by the rectangular hyperbolas $xy = 1$, $xy = 4$ and the lines $y = x + 1$, $y = x + 3$. [HINT: introduce the variables $u = xy$, $v = y - x$.]

12. Determine the volume of the part of the cylinder

$$x^2 + y^2 - 2ax = 0$$

cut off by the cylinder $z^2 = 2ax$.

13. Find the volume contained between the spheres
$x^2 + y^2 + x^2 = a^2$ and $x^2 + y^2 + z^2 = 4az$.

14. Find the volume which is common to the cone

$$a(b - z) = b(x^2 + y^2)^{\frac{1}{2}}$$

and the cylinder $x^2 + y^2 = ax$ and which is bounded by the plane $z = 0$.

15. Find the volume common to the three circular cylinders

$$x^2 + y^2 = a^2, \, y^2 + z^2 = a^2, \, z^2 + x^2 = a^2 \qquad (a > 0).$$

CHAPTER THREE
Surface Integrals

---

1. PRELIMINARY REMARKS ABOUT SURFACES

In this section we collect a few definitions and facts about surfaces. For details and proofs the reader should consult a textbook on Differential Geometry.*

A surface, S, is the set of points (x,y,z) in three-dimensional space whose coordinates are given by equations of the form

$$x = \xi(u,v),\ y = \eta(u,v),\ z = \zeta(u,v), \tag{1}$$

where the parameters u,v range over a region, D, of the (u,v)-plane. We may think of (1) as describing a mapping of D on to S. It will always be assumed that the functions ξ, η, ζ are continuous in D and that they are differentiable, save possibly at a finite number of points or on a finite number of arcs lying in D. A further condition of regularity, which is of a more technical nature, will be named presently. In the language of vectors we may say that a typical point of S is specified by the radius vector $\mathbf{r} = (x,y,z) = \mathbf{r}(u,v)$, expressing the fact that x, y and z are functions of u and v. (We are here indulging in the convenient, though slightly reprehensible, habit of using the same symbol for a function as for the values which the function attains.)

The mapping (1) transfers the features of D into corresponding features of S. For example, the set of straight lines $v = const = v_i$ $(i = 1,2, \ldots)$ becomes a family of curves $\mathbf{r} = \mathbf{r}(u,v_i)$ $(i = 1,2, \ldots)$, where the parameter u ranges over that part

*E.g. K. L. Wardle, *Differential Geometry* (in this series).

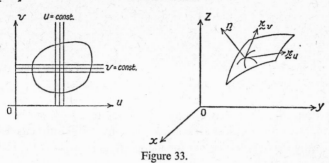

Figure 33.

of the line $v = v_i$ which lies in D. Similarly, we obtain a family of curves $\mathbf{r} = \mathbf{r}(u_i,v)$ ($i = 1,2, \ldots$) which are the images of the lines $u = u_i$ ($i = 1,2, \ldots$), the parameter now being v. These two families are called the *parametric curves*. Through each point $\mathbf{r}(u_0,v_0)$ of S there passes exactly one member of each family. The tangent vectors to the parametric curves at $\mathbf{r}(u_0,v_0)$ are

$$\mathbf{r}_u = \left(\frac{\partial x}{\partial u}, \frac{\partial y}{\partial u}, \frac{\partial z}{\partial u}\right)_0 \quad \text{and} \quad \mathbf{r}_v = \left(\frac{\partial x}{\partial v}, \frac{\partial y}{\partial v}, \frac{\partial z}{\partial v}\right)_0$$

respectively, where the suffix, 0, indicates that the partial derivatives are to be evaluated at the point (u_0, v_0) of D.

The normal to S at $\mathbf{r}(u_0,v_0)$ lies in the direction of the vector

$$\mathbf{r}_u \wedge \mathbf{r}_v = (A,B,C), \tag{2}$$

where $A = y_u z_v - y_v z_u = \dfrac{\partial(y,z)}{\partial(u,v)}$, $B = z_u x_v - z_v x_u = \dfrac{\partial(z,x)}{\partial(u,v)}$,

$C = x_u y_v - x_v y_u = \dfrac{\partial(x,y)}{\partial(u,v)}$ and all derivatives are to be evaluated at (u_0,v_0).

We say the point $\mathbf{r}(u_0,v_0)$ is *regular* if the functions ξ, η, ζ have continuous partial derivatives at (u_0,v_0) and satisfy the further condition that A,B,C do not vanish simultaneously, that is

$$A^2 + B^2 + C^2 > 0. \tag{3}$$

Henceforth we shall assume that the points of S are regular, possibly with the exception of a finite number of isolated points lying on a finite number of arcs. Also, in order to avoid complications we shall confine ourselves to *simple* surfaces, that is surfaces without self-intersections. This amounts to making the hypothesis that the mapping (1) is one-to-one. The following quantities are fundamental in the theory of surfaces.

$$E = \left(\frac{\partial x}{\partial u}\right)^2 + \left(\frac{\partial y}{\partial u}\right)^2 + \left(\frac{\partial z}{\partial u}\right)^2 = \mathbf{r}_u{}^2,$$

$$F = \frac{\partial x}{\partial u}\frac{\partial x}{\partial v} + \frac{\partial y}{\partial u}\frac{\partial y}{\partial v} + \frac{\partial z}{\partial u}\frac{\partial z}{\partial v} = \mathbf{r}_u.\mathbf{r}_v, \tag{4}$$

$$G = \left(\frac{\partial x}{\partial v}\right)^2 + \left(\frac{\partial y}{\partial v}\right)^2 + \left(\frac{\partial z}{\partial v}\right)^2 = \mathbf{r}_v{}^2.$$

The vector identity $(\mathbf{a} \wedge \mathbf{b}) = \mathbf{a}^2\mathbf{b}^2 - (\mathbf{a}.\mathbf{b})^2$ implies that

$$A^2 + B^2 + C^2 = EG - F^2. \tag{5}$$

At a regular point (u,v), this number is positive, and we shall put

$$\Delta = (EG - F^2)^{\frac{1}{2}} \quad (\Delta > 0). \tag{6}$$

The vector

$$\mathbf{n} = (\cos \alpha, \cos \beta, \cos \gamma) = \Delta^{-1}(A,B,C) \tag{7}$$

is called the† *unit normal* at (u,v).

According to our definition, a surface, S, is the image of a region, D, of the (u,v)-plane under the mapping (1). From a

† The definition is unambiguous as it stands, but it depends on the choice of parameters. For example, when u and v are interchanged, $\mathbf{n}$ is replaced by $-\mathbf{n}$, which could equally well be called the unit normal. For a closed surface it is customary to make $\mathbf{n}$ point towards the outside of S.

geometrical point of view, however, it is more natural to regard S as a set of points in the (x,y,z)-space, and it is then possible to have different parametric representations for the same surface. A change of parameters is expressed by an invertible transformation

$$u = \phi(p,q), \quad v = \psi(p,q), \tag{8}$$

where p and q are the new parameters. Hence the Jacobian of this transformation is non-zero, and without loss of generality we may assume that it is positive, thus

$$J = \frac{\partial(u,v)}{\partial(p,q)} > 0.$$

Let D^* be the region in the (p,q)-plane which corresponds to D under the transformation (8). The new parametric representation of S is then

$$\mathbf{r} = \mathbf{r}(\phi(p,q),\psi(p,q)),$$

where (p,q) ranges over D^*. The fundamental quantities for S must now be expressed in terms of p and q. Thus

$$A^* = \frac{\partial(y,z)}{\partial(p,q)} = \frac{\partial(y,z)}{\partial(u,v)} \frac{\partial(u,v)}{\partial(p,q)} = AJ,$$

where the asterisk denotes quantities in the (p,q)-system and, similarly, $B^* = BJ$, $C^* = CJ$, etc. In particular,

$$\Delta^* = (E^*G^* - F^{*2})^{\frac{1}{2}} = \Delta J. \tag{9}$$

When the surface is given by the Cartesian equation

$$z = \phi(x,y) \qquad ((x,y) \in D), \tag{10}$$

as in II, § 8, we may choose x and y as parameters and regard

$$x = x, \, y = y, \, z = \phi(x,y) \tag{11}$$

as the parametric representation of S. A simple calculation shows that in this case $A = -z_x$, $B = -z_y$, $C = 1$, and hence

$$\Delta = (1 + z_x^2 + z_y^2)^{\frac{1}{2}}. \tag{12}$$

SURFACE INTEGRALS

We note that, according to our convention, the normal makes an acute angle with the z-axis, because $C > 0$.

More generally, when S is defined by an implicit equation

$$F(x,y,z) = 0, \tag{13}$$

the normal vector is proportional to the vector

$$(F_x, F_y, F_z). \tag{14}$$

This can be verified by solving (13) for one of the variables and then using parametric equations analogous to (11), or by observing that (14) is tangential to every curve lying in S and passing through (x,y,z).

2. THE AREA OF A SURFACE

Up to now we have considered only areas of plane regions. The concept of area for a curved surface requires a new definition, and we shall use the following rough argument to make this definition plausible. Take four points P_i $(i = 1,2,3,4)$ on S whose position vectors are given by

$$\overrightarrow{OP_0} = \mathbf{r}(u,v), \ \overrightarrow{OP_1} = \mathbf{r}(u + h,v),$$
$$\overrightarrow{OP_2} = \mathbf{r}(u,v + k), \ \overrightarrow{OP_3} = \mathbf{r}(u + h,v + k)$$

respectively, where h and k are 'small' positive quantities.

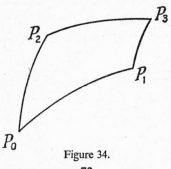

Figure 34.

72

Using Taylor's theorem and displaying only terms of the first order we find that

$$\overrightarrow{P_0P_1} = \mathbf{r}_u h + \ldots, \overrightarrow{P_0P_2} = \mathbf{r}_v k + \ldots, \overrightarrow{P_0P_3} = \mathbf{r}_u h + \mathbf{r}_v k + \ldots.$$

Hence, to a first approximation, $\overrightarrow{P_0P_3}$ is equal to $\overrightarrow{P_0P_1} + \overrightarrow{P_0P_2}$ and the quadrilateral is 'nearly' a parallelogram. As is known from vector algebra, the area of this parallelogram is

$$|P_0P_1 \wedge P_0P_2| = |\mathbf{r}_u \wedge \mathbf{r}_v|hk = (EG - F^2)^{\frac{1}{2}}hk.$$

It is customary to put $h = du, k = dv$ and to call the expression

$$dS = \Delta dudv = (EG - F^2)^{\frac{1}{2}}dudv \qquad (15)$$

the *element of area* of S. This leads to the definition

$$|S| = \iint_D (EG - F^2)^{\frac{1}{2}}dudv \qquad (16)$$

for the total area of S. We check that this expression is independent of the choice of parameters; for, by the rule for transforming a double integral,

$$\iint_D (EG - F^2)^{\frac{1}{2}}dudv = \iint_{D^*} (EG - F^2)^{\frac{1}{2}}J\, dpdq$$
$$= \iint_{D^*} (E^*G^* - F^{*2})^{\frac{1}{2}}dpdq.$$

On combining (7) and (15) we obtain the vector relation

$$\mathbf{n}\, dS = (\cos \alpha, \cos \beta, \cos \gamma)dS = (A,B,C)dudv. \qquad (17)$$

When the surface is given by the Cartesian equation

$$z = \phi(x,y),$$

we can use (12) and obtain the formula

$$dS = (1 + z_x^2 + z_y^2)^{\frac{1}{2}}dxdy \qquad (15)'$$

for the element of area and

$$|S| = \iint_D (1 + z_x^2 + z_y^2)^{\frac{1}{2}}dxdy \qquad (16)'$$

for the total area.

SURFACE INTEGRALS

Example 1. The surface of the sphere S: $x^2 + y^2 + z^2 = a^2$ may be represented by the equations

$$x = a \sin \theta \cos \phi, \quad y = a \sin \theta \sin \phi, \quad z = a \cos \theta, \quad (18)$$

where $D: 0 \leqslant \theta \leqslant \pi, 0 \leqslant \phi \leqslant 2\pi$. If P is an arbitrary point of the sphere, θ is the angle between OP and the positive

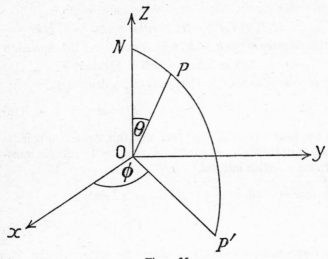

Figure 35.

z-direction. Let the circle of longitude through P meet the equatorial (x,y)-plane at P'. Then $OP' = a \sin \theta$, and ϕ is the angle which OP' makes with the positive x-direction. From (4) we find that

$$E = x_\theta{}^2 + y_\theta{}^2 + z_\theta{}^2 = a^2, \quad F = x_\theta x_\phi + y_\theta y_\phi + z_\theta z_\phi = 0,$$
$$G = x_\phi{}^2 + y_\phi{}^2 + z_\phi{}^2 = a^2 \sin \theta.$$

Hence the element of area of the sphere is

$$dS = (EG - F^2)^{\frac{1}{2}} d\phi d\theta = a^2 \sin \theta \, d\theta d\phi. \quad (19)$$

74

We observe that the North and South poles ($\theta = 0$ and $\theta = \pi$) are singular points in the parametric representations, but by an argument analogous to that used on p. 54, it can be shown that this does not invalidate the result obtained by integration, thus

$$|S| = \int\int_D a^2\sin\theta\, d\theta d\phi = \int_0^{2\pi} d\phi \int_0^\pi a^2\sin\theta\, d\theta = 4\pi a^2.$$

Example 2. Let $z = f(x)$ $(0 \leqslant \alpha \leqslant x \leqslant \beta)$ be the equation of a curve in the (x,z)-plane. If this curve rotates about the z-axis, it generates a surface of revolution, S, which can be represented by the equations

$$x = \rho\cos\theta, \quad y = \rho\sin\theta, \quad z = f(\rho), \tag{20}$$

where (ρ,θ) are polar coordinates in the (x,y)-plane. The parametric region is the rectangle D: $\alpha \leqslant \rho \leqslant \beta$, $0 \leqslant \theta \leqslant 2\pi$. We find that

$$E = x_\theta{}^2 + y_\theta{}^2 + z_\theta{}^2 = \rho^2,$$
$$F = x_\theta x_\rho + y_\theta y_\rho + z_\theta z_\rho = 0,$$
$$G = x_\rho{}^2 + y_\rho{}^2 + z_\rho{}^2 = 1 + (f'(\rho))^2.$$

Hence $(EG - F^2)^{\frac{1}{2}} = \rho\{1 + (f'(\rho))^2\}^{\frac{1}{2}}$ and

$$|S| = \int\int_D \rho\{1 + (f'(\rho))^2\}^{\frac{1}{2}}d\theta d\rho$$
$$= 2\pi\int_\alpha^\beta \rho\{1 + (f'(\rho))^2\}^{\frac{1}{2}}d\rho. \tag{21}$$

3. SURFACE INTEGRALS

Imagine a surface that is made of a thin material whose density at (x,y,z) is a function $f(x,y,z)$. This means that the mass of a surface element at (x,y,z) is equal to $f(x,y,z)dS$. Hence the total mass M of the shell is obtained by 'summing' the contributions from the various elements. The result is written as

$$M = \int\int_S f(x,y,z)dS \qquad (22)$$

and is called a *surface integral*. In order to evaluate this integral we use a parametric representation of S and express all quantities in terms of the parameters u,v. Thus, in the notation of (1) and (15),

$$f = f(\xi(u,v),\ \eta(u,v),\ \zeta(u,v))$$

and $dS = \Delta dudv$. Hence (21) is reduced to a double integral with respect to u and v, thus

$$\int\int_S f\, dS = \int\int_D f \Delta\, dudv. \qquad (23)$$

It is important to note that the value of the surface integral (21) does not depend on the choice of parameters. For if we make the transformation (8) to new parameters (p,q), then f is expressed in terms of p and q and $dudv$ becomes $\Delta J\, dpdq = \Delta^* dpdq$, whilst the region of integration is changed to D^*. Thus the integral on the right of (23) has the same form as before, except that the new parameters are used.

Example 3. Find the mass of a hemispherical shell whose density at P is proportional to the distance of P from the equatorial plane.

We may express the hemisphere by the equations (18), except that the parametric region is now $D: 0 \leqslant \theta \leqslant \tfrac{1}{2}\pi$, $0 \leqslant \phi \leqslant 2\pi$. The density at (x,y,z) is $f = kz = ka\cos\theta$. Hence, by (23),

$$M = \int\int_S f\, dS = \int\int_D ka\cos\theta\, a^2\sin\theta\, d\theta d\phi = \pi a^3 k.$$

The following type of surface integral is of great importance in Physics. Let P, Q and R be functions of sufficient regularity and consider the surface integral

$$N = \iint_S (P \cos \alpha + Q \cos \beta + R \cos \gamma)dS, \qquad (24)$$

where $\mathbf{n} = (\cos \alpha, \cos \beta, \cos \gamma)$ is the unit normal at an arbitrary point of S. If P, Q, R are the components of a vector $\mathbf{v} = (P,Q,R)$, then the integrand can be more briefly expressed as $\mathbf{v} \cdot \mathbf{n}$, which is the component of $\mathbf{v}$ in the direction of $\mathbf{n}$. The surface integral can be reduced to a double integral over the parametric region D by means of (17), thus

$$N = \iint_D (PA + QB + RC)dudv. \qquad (25)$$

We observe that the choice of parameters has no influence on the value of the integral. For, in the notation of p. 71, if we change to the (p,q)-system, the region of integration becomes D^* and the integrand has to be replaced by

$$(PA + QB + RC)J\,dpdq = (PA^* + QB^* + RC^*)dpdq,$$

which shows that the integral on the right of (25) might equally well have been referred to (p,q). It is therefore customary to omit all mention of parameters and to write

$$N = \iint_S (P\,dydz + Q\,dzdx + R\,dxdy), \qquad (26)$$

where the products of differentials are abbreviations for the following expressions:

$$\begin{aligned} dydz &= A\,dudv = \cos \alpha\,dS, \\ dzdx &= B\,dudv = \cos \beta\,dS, \\ dxdy &= C\,dudv = \cos \gamma\,dS. \end{aligned} \qquad (27)$$

The reader should note the difference between the present usage of the symbol $dxdy$ and that occurring in a (plane) double integral. Since C changes its sign when x and y are

SURFACE INTEGRALS

interchanged, we have here that $dydx = -dxdy$. As a rule, it is advisable to choose a convenient parametric representation for S and then to use the form (25) for N.

Example 4. Prove that if S is the ellipsoid

$$(x/a)^2 + (y/b)^2 + (z/c)^2 = 1,$$

$$\iint_S \left(\frac{dydz}{x} + \frac{dzdx}{y} + \frac{dxdy}{z} \right) = 4\pi \left(\frac{bc}{a} + \frac{ca}{b} + \frac{ab}{c} \right).$$

For reasons of symmetry, it is sufficient to consider one of the terms and to prove, for example, that

$$\iint_S \frac{dydz}{x} = 4\pi bc/a.$$

We use the parametric representation

$$x = a \sin \theta \cos \phi, \ y = b \sin \theta \sin \phi, \ z = c \cos \theta,$$

which has $D: 0 \leqslant \theta \leqslant \pi, \ 0 \leqslant \phi \leqslant 2\pi$ as parametric region. Now

$$A = \frac{\partial(y,z)}{\partial(\theta,\phi)} = \begin{vmatrix} b \cos \theta \sin \phi & b \sin \theta \cos \phi \\ -c \sin \theta & 0 \end{vmatrix} = bc \sin^2\theta \cos \phi.$$

Hence

$$\iint_S \frac{dydz}{x} = \iint_D \frac{bc \sin^2\theta \cos \phi}{a \sin \theta \cos \phi} d\theta d\phi = \frac{bc}{a} \iint_D \sin \theta \ d\theta d\phi$$

$$= \frac{bc}{a} \int_0^\pi \sin \theta \ d\theta \int_0^{2\pi} d\phi = 4\pi bc/a.$$

EXERCISES ON CHAPTER THREE

1. Show that the portion of the surface of the sphere $x^2 + y^2 + z^2 = a^2$ which lies inside the cylinder $x^2 + y^2 = ax$ has area $2\pi a^2$.
2. Find the area of the part of the surface $z^2 = 2xy$ which lies inside the sphere $x^2 + y^2 + z^2 = a^2$.

EXERCISES

3. Find the surface area of the '*torus*' $x = (a + b \cos u) \cos v$, $y = (a + b \cos u) \sin v$, $z = b \sin u (a > b, \ 0 \leqslant u \leqslant 2\pi, \ 0 \leqslant v \leqslant 2\pi)$, which is the surface generated by a circle of radius b moving at right angles to the (x,y)-plane in such a way that its centre describes the circle $x^2 + y^2 = a^2$.

4. Evaluate the surface integral $\iint_S z^2 dx dy$, where S is the sphere $x^2 + y^2 + z^2 = a^2$.

5. Evaluate $\iint_S x \, dS$, where S is that part of the surface of the paraboloid $z = 2 - (x^2 + y^2)$ for which $z \geqslant 0$.

6. Prove that $\iint_S \{x^2 + y^2 + (z - p)^2\}^{-\frac{1}{2}} dS$, where S is the surface of the sphere $x^2 + y^2 + z^2 = a^2 \ (a > 0)$, is equal to $4\pi a$, when $0 < p < a$, and is equal to $4\pi a^2/p$, when $p > a$.

CHAPTER FOUR
Volume Integrals

---

1. DEFINITION OF A VOLUME INTEGRAL

The treatment of volume, or triple, integrals is analogous to that of double integrals given in Chapter II. Most of the ideas that are required to develop the theory are straightforward extensions to a higher dimension. But the analysis becomes somewhat involved when written out in detail. We shall therefore confine ourselves to a brief description of the relevant results and illustrate them with a number of concrete examples.

The region of integration is now a set T in three-dimensional space. We assume that all such regions have a definite volume, denoted by $|T|$. When T is normal with respect to the z-axis, that is when T is defined by

$$T: \phi_2(x,y) \leqslant z \leqslant \phi_1(x,y), \quad (x,y) \in D \tag{1}$$

then $|T|$ is given by the formula established in II, § 8, namely

$$|T| = \iint_D (\phi_1 - \phi_2)dxdy.$$

The volume integral of a function $f(x,y,z)$ which is continuous in T, is defined as follows. Make a *partition*

$$\Delta: \tau_1, \tau_2, \ldots, \tau_n$$

of T and define the *norm*, v, of Δ as the smallest number such that every τ_i can be enclosed in a sphere of radius v.

Choose a point (x_i, y_i, z_i) in τ_i and form the approximation sum

$$S(\Delta) = \sum_{i=1}^{n} f(x_i, y_i, z_i)|\tau_i|.$$

Let Δ run through a set of partitions such that ν tends to zero. Then it can be shown that $S(\Delta)$ tends to a limit which is independent of the choice of the points (x_i, y_i, z_i), and we write

$$\lim_{\nu \to 0} S(\Delta) = \iiint_T f(x,y,z)dxdydz. \tag{2}$$

This is the *Existence Theorem* for volume integrals. The theorem still holds when f is discontinuous, but bounded, along a finite number of surfaces lying in T. The formal rules (i) to (v), enunciated for double integrals on p. 24, apply with the obvious modifications. In particular, we mention the formula for the volume

$$|T| = \iiint_T dxdydz, \tag{3}$$

which is an immediate consequence of the definition, and we note the important inequality

$$\left| \iiint_T f\, dxdydz \right| \leqslant \iiint_T |f|dxdydz. \tag{4}$$

2. REDUCTION TO REPEATED INTEGRAL

Suppose that T is normal with respect to the z-axis, as shown in Fig. 36. Then we have the reduction formula

$$\iiint_T f\, dxdydz = \iint_D dxdy \int_{\phi_2(x,y)}^{\phi_1(x,y)} f(x,y,z)dz. \tag{5}$$

This means that the volume integral may be found by the

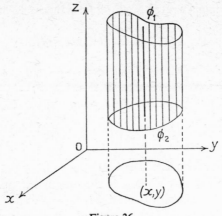

Figure 36.

following process. For fixed (x,y) evaluate the ordinary integral

$$\int_{\phi_2}^{\phi_1} f(x,y,z)dz = g(x,y),$$

where the limits are in general functions of x and y, namely the equations of the surfaces which bound T on top and bottom.

Then evaluate the double integral $\iint_D g(x,y)dxdy$, the region of integration being the common projection of the two surfaces $z = \phi_1(x,y)$ and $z = \phi_2(x,y)$ on the (x,y)-plane

When P is a parallelepiped with edges parallel to the axes, given by

$$P: \alpha \leqslant x \leqslant a, \quad \beta \leqslant y \leqslant b, \quad \gamma \leqslant z \leqslant c, \tag{6}$$

then the limits of integration are constant and the reduction formula takes the form

$$\iiint_P f \, dxdydz = \int_\alpha^a dx \int_\beta^b dy \int_\gamma^c f \, dz. \tag{7}$$

82

The result is further simplified if, in addition, the integrand is a product of functions each involving only one of the variables, say

$$f(x,y,z) = F(x)G(y)H(z).$$

Then the integral becomes

$$\iiint_P FGH \, dxdydz = \left(\int_\alpha^a F \, dx\right)\left(\int_\beta^b G \, dy\right)\left(\int_\gamma^c H \, dz\right). \quad (8)$$

It need hardly be pointed out that analogous reduction formulae exist for regions which are normal with respect to the x-axis or y-axis. If a region is normal with respect to more than one axis, as for example a parallelepiped, then we have a choice of several reduction formulae.

Example 1. Evaluate $\iiint_P (x - y + z)dxdydz$, where

$$P: 1 \leqslant x \leqslant 2, \quad 2 \leqslant y \leqslant 3, \quad 1 \leqslant z \leqslant 3.$$

Using (7) we find that the integral is equal to

$$\int_1^2 dx \int_2^3 dy \int_1^3 (x - y + z)dz = \int_1^2 dx \int_2^3 dy \left[xz - yz + \tfrac{1}{2}z^2\right]_1^3$$

$$= \int_1^2 dx \int_2^3 (2x - 2y + 4)dy = \int_1^2 dx \left[2xy - y^2 + 4y\right]_2^3$$

$$= \int_1^2 (2x - 1)dx = 2.$$

Example 2. Evaluate $\iiint_T x^2y^2z \, dxdydz$, where T is the portion of the cone $x^2 + y^2 = xz$ which lies between the planes $z = 0$ and $z = c$ $(c > 0)$.

The region T is normal with respect to the z-axis. It is bounded by the plane $\phi_1: z = c$ on the top and by the surface $\phi_2: z = (x^2 + y^2)/x$ at the bottom. The projection of T on the (x,y)-plane is the region D which is bounded by the circle $\gamma: x^2 + y^2 = cx$. It is convenient to introduce polar coordinates in the $(x,y,)$-plane: $x = r \cos \theta$, $y = r \sin \theta$. Then

$$\phi_2: z = r/\cos \theta \quad \text{and} \quad \gamma: r = c \cos \theta \quad (-\pi/2 \leqslant \theta \leqslant \pi/2).$$

Hence the integral becomes

$$\iint_D r^4\cos^2\theta \sin^2\theta \, rdrd\theta \int_{\phi_2}^{\phi_1} z \, dz$$

$$= \iint_D r^4\cos^2\theta \sin^2\theta \, rdrd\theta \left(\tfrac{1}{2}\phi_1^2 - \tfrac{1}{2}\phi_2^2 \right)$$

$$= \tfrac{1}{2}\int_{-\pi/2}^{\pi/2} d\theta \int_0^{c \cos \theta} (c^2r^5\cos^2\theta \sin^2\theta - r^7\sin^2\theta)dr$$

$$= \int_0^{\pi/2} (\tfrac{1}{6}c^8\cos^8\theta \sin^2\theta - \tfrac{1}{8} c^8\cos^8\theta \sin^2\theta)d\theta$$

$$= \frac{c^8}{24}\int_0^{\pi/2} (\cos^8\theta - \cos^{10}\theta)d\theta = \frac{7\pi}{48}\left(\frac{c}{2}\right)^8 \text{(see } IC, \text{ p. 83 (33))} \cdot$$

3. GAUSS'S THEOREM (DIVERGENCE THEOREM)

Let T be a three-dimensional region which is normal with respect to the z-axis (see Fig. 36). We denote the boundary of T by S. This is a closed surface which consists of three parts, namely (i) $z = \phi_1(x,y)$ (the top of T), (ii) $z = \phi_2(x,y)$ (the bottom of T) and (iii) the cylindrical surface, Z, with cross-section D and generators parallel to the z-axis.

Gauss's Theorem is the three-dimensional analogue of Green's Theorem (p. 37), and in its simplest form is concerned with an integral of the type

$$\iiint_T \frac{\partial R}{\partial z}dxdydz, \tag{9}$$

where $R = R(x,y,z)$ is an arbitrary function with continuous partial derivatives. By the reduction formula (7) we immediately deduce that

$$\iiint_T \frac{\partial R}{\partial z}\,dxdydz = \iint_D dxdy \int_{\phi_2}^{\phi_1} \frac{\partial R}{\partial z}dz$$

$$= \iint_D \{R(x,y,\phi_1) - R(x,y,\phi_2)\}dxdy. \quad (10)$$

We shall now show that the integral on the right is equal to the surface integral $\iint_S R\,dxdy$. Since the three parts of S will have to be treated separately, we write

$$\iint_S R\,dxdy = \iint_{\phi_1} R\,dxdy + \iint_{\phi_2} R\,dxdy + \iint_Z R\,dxdy. \quad (11)$$

For each of the partial surfaces we shall select a convenient parametric representation and in accordance with III(27) replace $dxdy$ by $C\,dudv = \cos\gamma\,\Delta dudv$, where $(\cos\alpha, \cos\beta, \cos\gamma)$ is the outward-drawn unit normal vector to S at the point $\mathbf{r}(u,v)$. (i) For the surface ϕ_1 we can take x, y as parameters. The parametric region is then D, and $C = 1$ (see p. 71); also, on ϕ_1, $R = R(x,y,\phi_1)$. Hence

$$\iint_{\phi_1} R\,dxdy = \iint_D R(x,y,\phi_1)dxdy.$$

(ii) For the surface ϕ_2 we can again choose x,y as parameters, but in this case $C = -1$, because the outward-drawn normal to S on ϕ_2 makes an obtuse angle with the z-axis; again, on ϕ_2, $R = R(x,y,\phi_2)$, and

$$\iint_{\phi_2} R\,dxdy = -\iint_D R(x,y,\phi_2)dxdy.$$

(iii) As regards Z, we need only observe that the normal to S on Z is perpendicular to the z-axis, so that the scalar product of the vectors $(\cos \alpha, \cos \beta, \cos \gamma)$ and $(0,0,1)$ is zero. It follows that $\cos \gamma = 0$, and this implies that the last term in (11) vanishes.

Hence on comparing (10) and (11) we find that

$$\iiint_T \frac{\partial R}{\partial z} dxdydz = \iint_S R \, dxdy. \qquad (12)$$

If T is normal with respect to each of the axes, we can obtain analogous formulae by cyclically interchanging x,y,z. On adding these results we have the following theorem.

Theorem (Gauss's Theorem or Divergence Theorem). *Let T be a three-dimensional region which is normal with respect to each of the axes, and let P, Q, R be continuous functions in T such that $\partial P/\partial x$, $\partial Q/\partial y$ and $\partial R/\partial z$ are also continuous. Then*

$$\iiint_T \left(\frac{\partial P}{\partial x} + \frac{\partial Q}{\partial y} + \frac{\partial R}{\partial z} \right) dxdydz$$

$$= \iint_S P \, dydz + Q \, dzdx + R \, dxdy, \qquad (13)$$

where S is the boundary of T.

Remarks 1. Using (III, 27) we can express this result as

$$\iiint_T \left(\frac{\partial P}{\partial x} + \frac{\partial Q}{\partial y} + \frac{\partial R}{\partial z} \right) dxdydz$$

$$= \iint_S (P \cos \alpha + Q \cos \beta + R \cos \gamma) dS. \qquad (14)$$

2. The formula (14) is the generalization of (II, 26) (p. 41) and not of (II, 22) (p. 38). This explains the fact that no minus signs appear on the right-hand side.

3. We have established the theorem only for the case in which T is normal with respect to all three axes, but the result holds more generally when T is the union of a finite number of normal regions.

4. If **F** is a vector with components P, Q, R along the coordinate axes, the function

$$\text{div } \mathbf{F} = \frac{\partial P}{\partial x} + \frac{\partial Q}{\partial y} + \frac{\partial R}{\partial z}$$

is called the *divergence* of **F**. The integrand on the right of (14) can then be expressed as $(\mathbf{F}.\mathbf{n})$ and the formula can be written more concisely as

$$\iiint_T \text{div } \mathbf{F} \, dxdydz = \iint_S \mathbf{F}.\mathbf{n} \, dS. \tag{15}$$

This explains the term *divergence theorem*.

When T is normal with respect to the three coordinate axes, we can express the volume of T as a surface integral in three ways by putting in turn $P = x$, $Q = 0$, $R = 0$; $P = 0$, $Q = y$, $R = 0$; $P = 0$, $Q = 0$, $R = z$. In each case the integral on the left of (13) becomes $\iiint_T dxdydz = |T|$. Thus

$$|T| = \iint_S x \, dydz = \iint_S y \, dzdx = \iint_S z \, dxdy. \tag{16}$$

Example 3. If p is the length of the perpendicular from the centre on to a tangent plane of an ellipsoid, S, whose semi-axes are a, b, c, show that

$$\iint_S \frac{dS}{p} = \frac{4\pi}{3} abc\left(\frac{1}{a^2} + \frac{1}{b^2} + \frac{1}{c^2}\right). \tag{17}$$

The equation of the ellipsoid is

$$\phi = (x/a)^2 + (y/b)^2 + (z/c)^2 - 1 = 0.$$

The tangent plane at (x,y,z) is given by

$$(X - x)/a^2 + (Y - y)/b^2 + (Z - z)/c^2 = 1,$$

where (X,Y,Z) are the coordinates of an arbitrary point on the tangent plane. This equation must be proportional to

87

VOLUME INTEGRALS

the 'perpendicular form' $X \cos \alpha + Y \cos \beta + Z \cos \gamma = p$, whence

$$x/a^2 = \cos \alpha /p, \quad y/b^2 = \cos \beta /p, \quad z/c = \cos \gamma /p.$$

We have therefore that

$$x \cos \alpha /a^2 + y \cos \beta /b^2 + z \cos \gamma /p$$
$$= (\cos^2\alpha + \cos^2\beta + \cos^2\gamma)/p = 1/p.$$

Thus

$$\iint_S \frac{dS}{p} = \iint_S \left(\frac{x}{a^2} \cos \alpha + \frac{y}{b^2} \cos \beta + \frac{z}{c^2} \cos \gamma \right) dS$$
$$= \iiint_T \left(\frac{1}{a^2} + \frac{1}{b^2} + \frac{1}{c^2}\right) dx dy dz,$$

by (14). The result now follows because the last integrand is constant and the volume of T is $\dfrac{4\pi}{3} abc$ (see Example 4, p. 92).

4. CHANGE OF VARIABLES

The introduction of new variables u, v, w is accomplished by an invertible mapping

$$\mu: x = p_1(u,v,w), \; y = p_2(u,v,w), \; z = p_3(u,v,w) \qquad (18)$$

from the (u,v,w)-space into the (x,y,z)-space. The functions p_1, p_2 and p_3 are assumed to be differentiable. If the region T^* corresponds to the region T under μ, the Jacobian

$$J = \frac{\partial(x,y,z)}{\partial(u,v,w)} = \begin{vmatrix} \dfrac{\partial x}{\partial u} & \dfrac{\partial x}{\partial v} & \dfrac{\partial x}{\partial w} \\[2mm] \dfrac{\partial y}{\partial u} & \dfrac{\partial y}{\partial v} & \dfrac{\partial y}{\partial w} \\[2mm] \dfrac{\partial z}{\partial u} & \dfrac{\partial z}{\partial v} & \dfrac{\partial z}{\partial w} \end{vmatrix} \qquad (19)$$

must be non-zero in T^*, and there is no loss of generality in supposing that

$$J > 0. \tag{20}$$

When μ is followed by another mapping

$$v: \quad u = q_1(\xi,\eta,\zeta), \quad v = q_2(\xi,\eta,\zeta), \quad w = q_3(\xi,\eta,\zeta),$$

the resulting mapping from ξ, η, ζ to x, y, z has the Jacobian

$$\frac{\partial(x,y,z)}{\partial(\xi,\eta,\zeta)} = \frac{\partial(x,y,z)}{\partial(u,v,w)} \frac{\partial(u,v,w)}{\partial(\xi,\eta,\zeta)} \tag{21}$$

whence by taking $\xi = x, \quad \eta = y, \quad z = \zeta,$

$$\frac{\partial(u,v,w)}{\partial(x,y,z)} = 1 \left/ \frac{\partial(x,y,z)}{\partial(u,v,w)} \right. . \tag{22}$$

The procedure for transforming a volume integral is analogous to that for a double integral discussed in II, §§ 5–6. The main step is to establish a formula for the 'element of volume'. As one would expect, the result is that, in an arbitrary coordinate system, the element of volume is

$$J \, dudvdw. \tag{23}$$

A proof of (23) could be given similar to that in Chapter II, but we shall here merely outline a rough argument which

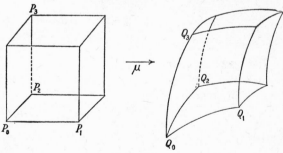

Figure 37.

serves to make (23) plausible. We start with a 'small' parallelepiped, Π, in the (u,v,w)-space which has one of its vertices at an arbitrary point $P_0 = (u,v,w)$. Let the vertices adjacent to P_0 be $P_1 = (u + du,v,w), P_2 = (u,v + dv,w), P_3 = (u,v,w + dw)$. The mapping μ transfers this parallelepiped into a region, $\mu\Pi$, which is bounded by curved surfaces, and it is the volume of $\mu\Pi$, evaluated to the first approximation, which gives the required element. Let $\mu P_i = Q_i = (x_i, y_i, z_i)$ $(i = 0,1,2,3)$. Going back to the definition (18) of μ we find that $x_0 = p_1(u,v,w)$, $x_1 = p_1(u + du,v,w)$, $x_2 = p_1(u,v + dv,w)$, $x_3 = p_1(u,v,w + dw)$, and similar expressions hold for y_i and z_i. Hence, to a first approximation,

$$x_1 - x_0 = (\partial x/\partial u)du,$$
$$x_2 - x_0 = (\partial x/\partial v)dv,$$
$$x_3 - x_0 = (\partial x/\partial w)dw, \text{ etc.}$$

Now it turns out that, for the degree of accuracy demanded, it suffices to replace $\mu\Pi$ by the parallelepiped spanned by the vectors $\overrightarrow{Q_0 Q_i}$ $(i = 1,2,3)$. Using the familiar formula from solid geometry, we conclude that the volume of this parallelepiped is equal to

$$\begin{vmatrix} x_1 - x_0 & y_1 - y_0 & z_1 - z_0 \\ x_2 - x_0 & y_2 - y_0 & z_2 - z_0 \\ x_3 - x_0 & y_3 - y_0 & z_3 - z_0 \end{vmatrix} = J\,dudvdw,$$

to the first approximation.

We shall now mention a few examples of transformations.

(i) In the linear transformation

$$\left. \begin{array}{l} x = a_0 + a_1u + a_2v + a_3w \\ y = b_0 + b_1u + b_2v + b_3w \\ z = c_0 + c_1u + c_2v + c_3w \end{array} \right\} \tag{24}$$

the Jacobian is

$$J = \begin{vmatrix} a_1 & a_2 & a_3 \\ b_1 & b_2 & b_3 \\ c_1 & c_2 & c_3 \end{vmatrix},$$

which must be assumed to be non-zero, and, indeed, positive according to our convention.

(ii) The transformation to cylindrical polar coordinates, with the z-axis as axis of symmetry, is given by the equations

$$x = \rho \cos \phi, \; y = \rho \sin \phi, \; z = z, \qquad (25)$$

where ρ is the perpendicular distance of the point $P = (x,y,z)$ from the z-axis and (ρ,ϕ) are the polar coordinates of the projection $P' = (x,y)$ of P on to the (x,y)-plane. The computation of the Jacobian is virtually the same as that for plane polar coordinates (p. 44), and it is found that

$$\frac{\partial(x,y,z)}{\partial(\rho,\phi,z)} = \rho.$$

(iii) Spherical polar coordinates (r,θ,ϕ) are related to Cartesian coordinates by the equations (see III (18), p. 74),

$$x = r \sin \theta \cos \phi, \quad y = r \sin \theta \sin \phi, \quad z = r \cos \theta, \quad (26)$$

where $r \geqslant 0$, $0 \leqslant \theta \leqslant \pi$, $0 \leqslant \phi \leqslant 2\pi$. The Jacobian

$$\partial(x,y,z)/\partial(r,\theta,\phi)$$

can either be calculated directly from the definition or by the observation that the transformation (26) can be regarded as the resultant of (25) followed by the transformation

$$\rho = r \sin \theta, \; z = r \cos \theta, \; \phi = \phi,$$

which has the Jacobian $\partial(\rho,\phi,z)/\partial(r,\theta,\phi) = r$. Hence

$$\frac{\partial(x,y,z)}{\partial(r,\theta,\phi)} = \frac{\partial(x,y,z)}{\partial(\rho,\phi,z)} \cdot \frac{\partial(\rho,\phi,z)}{\partial(r,\theta,\phi)} = \rho r,$$

VOLUME INTEGRALS

that is

$$\frac{\partial(x,y,z)}{\partial(r,\theta,\phi)} = r^2\sin\theta. \tag{27}$$

We note that the transformation becomes irregular when $r = 0$ or $\theta = 0$ or $\theta = \pi$.

Example 4. Find the volume of the ellipsoid

$$E: (x/a)^2 + (y/b)^2 + (z/c)^2 \leqslant 1.$$

It is convenient to make a preliminary transformation $x = a\xi$, $y = b\eta$, $z = c\zeta$, which maps E onto the solid unit sphere $I: \xi^2 + \eta^2 + \zeta^2 \leqslant 1$. The Jacobian of this linear transformation is abc, so that

$$|E| = \iiint_E dxdydz = \iiint_{E_0} abc\, d\xi d\eta d\zeta = abc|I|,$$

and if we are unwilling to invoke the elementary formula $|I| = \frac{4}{3}\pi$, we can proceed by using spherical polar coordinates to find that

$$|I| = \int_0^1 dr \int_0^{2\pi} d\phi \int_0^{\pi} r^2\sin\theta\, d\theta$$
$$= \left(\int_0^1 r^2 dr\right)\left(\int_0^{2\pi} d\phi\right)\left(\int_0^{\pi} \sin\theta\, d\theta\right) = \frac{4\pi}{3}.$$

Example 5. Evaluate

$$\iiint_I (\lambda x + \mu y + \nu z)^{2n} dxdydz,$$

where n is a positive integer and $I: x^2 + y^2 + z^2 \leqslant 1$.

We observe that if

$$R = \begin{pmatrix} \alpha_1 & \beta_1 & \gamma_1 \\ \alpha_2 & \beta_2 & \gamma_2 \\ \alpha_3 & \beta_3 & \gamma_3 \end{pmatrix}$$

92

is an orthogonal matrix of determinant unity, then the linear transformation

$$\xi = \alpha_1 x + \beta_1 y + \gamma_1 z,$$
$$\eta = \alpha_2 x + \beta_2 y + \gamma_2 z,$$
$$\zeta = \alpha_3 x + \beta_3 y + \gamma_3 z$$

has a Jacobian equal to unity and maps I into the region

$$K: \xi^2 + \eta^2 + \zeta^2 \leqslant 1.$$

We may choose for $(\alpha_3, \beta_3, \gamma_3)$ any unit vector, in particular the vector $\sigma(\lambda, \mu, \nu)$ where $\sigma = (\lambda^2 + \mu^2 + \nu^2)^{-\frac{1}{2}}$. For the first two rows of R we can take any two unit vectors which are orthogonal to each other and to $(\alpha_3, \beta_3, \gamma_3)$, and it is clearly possible to arrange that $\det R = 1$. Having constructed R in this way, we note that $\zeta = \sigma(\lambda x + \mu y + \nu z)$. Finally, we replace ξ, η, ζ by spherical polar coordinates. Thus the integral becomes

$$\sigma^{-2n} \int\!\!\int\!\!\int_K \zeta^{2n} d\xi d\eta d\zeta = \sigma^{-2n} \int_0^1 dr \int_0^{2\pi} d\phi \int_0^{\pi} r^{2n} \cos^{2n}\theta \, r^2 \sin\theta \, d\theta$$

$$= \sigma^{-2n} \int_0^1 r^{2n+2} dr \int_0^{2\pi} d\phi \int_0^{\pi} \cos^{2n}\theta \sin\theta \, d\theta$$

$$= \frac{4\pi(\lambda^2 + \mu^2 + \nu^2)^n}{(2n+3)(2n+1)}.$$

5. STOKES'S THEOREM

Let Γ be a closed (in general, twisted) curve in space and let S be an (open) surface having Γ as boundary. Then the simplest form of Stokes's Theorem states that

$$\int_{\Gamma} P \, dx = \int\!\!\int_S \left(\frac{\partial P}{\partial z} \cos\beta - \frac{\partial P}{\partial y} \cos\gamma \right) dS, \qquad (28)$$

where $P = P(x,y,z)$ is a continuous function with continuous derivatives $\partial P/\partial z$ and $\partial P/\partial y$. The orientation of Γ and of the unit normal $(\cos \alpha, \cos \beta, \cos \gamma)$ of S will be specified presently. We assume that S has a parametric representation

$$\mu: \quad x = \xi(u,v), \quad y = \eta(u,v), \quad z = \zeta(u,v), \qquad (29)$$

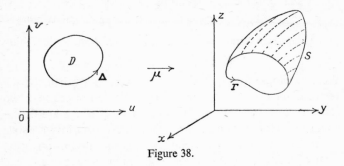

Figure 38.

in which the functions ξ, η, ζ possess partial derivatives up to the second order. Let D be the parametric region and let Δ be the boundary of D, that is $\mu D = S$, $\mu\Delta = \Gamma$. As usual, we assume that Δ is described in the counter-clockwise sense. This orientation is then transferred to Γ, and it is this orientation that will be used for the evaluation of the line integral on the left of (28). For the components of the normal we use III, (17), thereby fixing the orientation of this vector. In particular, $\cos \beta\, dS = \dfrac{\partial(z,x)}{\partial(u,v)} du\, dv$, $\cos \gamma\, dS = \dfrac{\partial(x,y)}{\partial(u,v)} du\, dv$. Since we are concerned only with points on Γ and S, we can regard P as a function of u and v. Finally, the parametric representation of Γ is induced by that of Δ with the aid of μ, so that the relation $dx = \dfrac{\partial x}{\partial u} du + \dfrac{\partial x}{\partial v} dv$ holds on Γ. Thus both sides of (28) can be expressed in terms of u and v, and indeed our assertion

94

is equivalent to the equation

$$\int_\Delta P\frac{\partial x}{\partial u}du + P\frac{\partial x}{\partial v}dv = \iint_D \left(\frac{\partial P}{\partial z}\frac{\partial(z,x)}{\partial(u,v)} - \frac{\partial P}{\partial y}\frac{\partial(x,y)}{\partial(u,v)}\right)du\,dv, \quad (30)$$

which we shall now proceed to prove. First, we shall rewrite the integrand on the right by using the formal identity

$$\frac{\partial P}{\partial z}\frac{\partial(z,y)}{\partial(u,v)} - \frac{\partial P}{\partial y}\frac{\partial(x,y)}{\partial(u,v)} = \frac{\partial P}{\partial u}\frac{\partial x}{\partial v} - \frac{\partial P}{\partial v}\frac{\partial x}{\partial u}, \quad (31)$$

which is easily verified. In fact, the expression on the right is equal to

$$\left(\frac{\partial P}{\partial x}\frac{\partial x}{\partial u} + \frac{\partial P}{\partial y}\frac{\partial y}{\partial u} + \frac{\partial P}{\partial z}\frac{\partial z}{\partial u}\right)\frac{\partial x}{\partial v} - \left(\frac{\partial P}{\partial x}\frac{\partial x}{\partial v} + \frac{\partial P}{\partial y}\frac{\partial y}{\partial v} + \frac{\partial P}{\partial z}\frac{\partial z}{\partial v}\right)\frac{\partial x}{\partial u}$$

$$= \frac{\partial P}{\partial z}\frac{\partial(z,x)}{\partial(u,v)} - \frac{\partial P}{\partial y}\frac{\partial(x,y)}{\partial(u,v)},$$

as required. Therefore, (30) is equivalent to

$$\int_\Delta P\frac{\partial x}{\partial u}du + P\frac{\partial x}{\partial v}dv = \iint_D \left(\frac{\partial P}{\partial u}\frac{\partial x}{\partial v} - \frac{\partial P}{\partial v}\frac{\partial x}{\partial u}\right)du\,dv. \quad (32)$$

However, this is an almost immediate consequence of Green's Theorem (II, p. 37), which tells us that the line integral on the left is equal to

$$\iint_D \left\{\frac{\partial}{\partial u}\left(P\frac{\partial x}{\partial v}\right) - \frac{\partial}{\partial v}\left(P\frac{\partial x}{\partial u}\right)\right\}du\,dv$$

$$= \iint_D \left(\frac{\partial P}{\partial u}\frac{\partial x}{\partial v} - \frac{\partial P}{\partial v}\frac{\partial x}{\partial u}\right)du\,dv.$$

This completes the proof of (30) and hence of (28).

Analogous relations can be established by a cyclic permutation of the variables x, y and z, and by the introduction of two further functions, Q and R. On adding the formulae so obtained, we can write the final result in the following form:

VOLUME INTEGRALS

Theorem (Stokes's Theorem). *Let Γ be a closed curve in space and let S be a surface having Γ as boundary. Then*

$$\int_\Gamma P\,dx + Q\,dy + R\,dz = \iint_S \left\{ \left(\frac{\partial R}{\partial y} - \frac{\partial Q}{\partial z} \right) \cos\alpha \right.$$
$$\left. + \left(\frac{\partial P}{\partial z} - \frac{\partial R}{\partial x} \right) \cos\beta + \left(\frac{\partial Q}{\partial x} - \frac{\partial P}{\partial y} \right) \cos\gamma \right\} dS, \quad (33)$$

where $(\cos\alpha, \cos\beta, \cos\gamma)$ is the normal to S, suitably orientated.

It is an immediate consequence of this theorem that

$$\int_\Gamma P\,dx + Q\,dy + R\,dz = 0 \quad (34)$$

for an arbitrary simple closed curve Γ provided that

$$\frac{\partial R}{\partial y} = \frac{\partial Q}{\partial z}, \quad \frac{\partial P}{\partial z} = \frac{\partial R}{\partial x}, \quad \frac{\partial Q}{\partial x} = \frac{\partial P}{\partial y}. \quad (35)$$

The equations (35) are certainly satisfied if there exists a function $V = V(x,y,z)$ such that

$$P = \frac{\partial V}{\partial x}, \, Q = \frac{\partial V}{\partial y}, \, R = \frac{\partial V}{\partial z}. \quad (36)$$

But in this case, the validity of (34) is anyhow obvious from an extension of the argument given on p. 11.

EXERCISES ON CHAPTER FOUR

1. Evaluate $\iiint_R (x - y + z)dxdydz$, where R is the parallelepiped defined by $1 \leqslant x \leqslant 2$, $2 \leqslant y \leqslant 3$, $1 \leqslant z \leqslant 3$.

2. Evaluate $\iiint_E \exp\{(x/a)^2 + (y/b)^2 + (z/c)^2\}^{\frac{1}{2}}dxdydz$, where E is the interior of the ellipsoid $(x/a)^2 + (y/b)^2 + (z/c)^2 \leqslant 1$.

EXERCISES

3. Evaluate $\iiint_T (x^3 + y^3 + z^3)dxdydz$, where T is the interior

of the sphere $x^2 + y^2 + z^2 - 2a(x + y + z) + 2a^2 = 0$.

4. Prove *Dirichlet's formula*

$$\iiint_T x^\alpha y^\beta z^\gamma f(x + y + z)dxdydz$$
$$= \frac{\alpha!\beta!\gamma!}{(\alpha + \beta + \gamma + 2)!}\int_0^1 t^{\alpha+\beta+\gamma+2}f(t)dt,$$

where α, β, and γ are greater than -1 and T is the tetrahedron defined by $x \geqslant 0$, $y \geqslant 0$, $z \geqslant 0$, $x + y + x \leqslant 1$.

[HINT: the volume integral is equal to $\iint_D x^\alpha y^\beta F(x + y)dxdy$,

where $D: x \geqslant 0, y \geqslant 0, x + y \leqslant 1$, and $F(s) = \int_0^{1-s} z^\gamma f(s + z)dz$.

Use II, (43) to evaluate the integral over D and apply this formula again to obtain a single integral.]

5. Show that $\iiint_T (x^2 + y^2 + z^2)dxdydz = a^5/20$, where T is the

tetrahedron bounded by the planes $x = 0$, $y = 0$, $z = 0$, $x + y + z = a$ $(a > 0)$.

6. Evaluate $\iiint_E \{(x/a)^2 + (y/b)^2 + (z/c)^2\}x^2y^2z^2dxdydz$, where

$E: (x/a)^2 + (y/b)^2 + (z/c)^2 \leqslant 1$.

7. Prove that $\iint_S p(x^2 + y^2 + z^2)dS = 4\pi abc(a^2 + b^2 + c^2)/3$,

where S is the surface $(x/a)^2 + (y/b)^2 + (z/c)^2 = 1$ and p is the length of the perpendicular from the origin to the tangent plane at (x,y,z).

8. Show that the volume bounded by $(x/a)^2 + (y/b)^2 + (z/c)^{2n} = 1$ is $4n\pi abc/(2n + 1)$.

9. Prove that, if $\rho = (\xi^2 + \eta^2 + \zeta^2)^{\frac{1}{2}}$ and T is the sphere
$$x^2 + y^2 + z^2 \leqslant a^2 \ (a > 0),$$

then $\displaystyle\iiint_T \{(x - \xi)^2 + (y - \eta)^2 + (z - \xi)^2\}^{-\frac{1}{2}}dxdydz$

is equal to $4\pi a^3/3$ when $\rho > a$ and is equal to $2\pi(3a^2 - \rho^2)/3$, when $\rho < a$.

[HINT: without loss of generality it may be assued that, after a suitable rotation of axes, $\xi = \eta = 0$, $\zeta = \rho$.]

10. Verify Stokes's Theorem when S is the hemisphere
$$x^2 + y^2 + z^2 = a^2, z \geqslant 0 \text{ and } P = -y, Q = x, R = 0.$$

11. Find the value of k for which
$$\iint_S \{kz \cos \alpha + (3x^2 - kyz) \cos \beta + (1 + z^2) \cos \gamma\}dS = 0,$$

where S is an arbitrary closed surface.

12. Prove that, for any closed surface,
$$\iint_S \left\{ \left(\frac{\partial R}{\partial y} - \frac{\partial Q}{\partial z}\right) \cos \alpha + \left(\frac{\partial P}{\partial z} - \frac{\partial R}{\partial x}\right) \cos \beta \right.$$
$$\left. + \left(\frac{\partial Q}{\partial x} - \frac{\partial P}{\partial y}\right) \cos \gamma \right\}dS = 0.$$

Appendix

In order to establish the formula (19) of p. 32 we introduce a function f^* which serves essentially the same purpose as f_D defined in (16), p. 31, but has the property that it is continuous in R.

Let D be the region given by

$$D: \quad a \leqslant x \leqslant b, \quad \psi(x) \leqslant y \leqslant \phi(x),$$

which is normal relative to the x-axis and suppose that f is continuous in D. Choose an arbitrary (small) positive number ε and construct the additional arcs $y = \phi(x) + \varepsilon, y = \psi(x) - \varepsilon$. Thus D is extended by two bands B_1, B_2. Enclose the extended

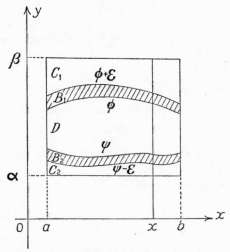

Figure 39.

region in a rectangle $R: a \leqslant x \leqslant b, \alpha \leqslant y \leqslant \beta$. The rectangle R now appears as the union of the non-overlapping regions D, B_1, B_2, C_1, C_2 as shown in Fig. 38. Define the function f^* by the following rule

$$f^* = \begin{cases} f, \text{ if } (x,y) \, \varepsilon \, D \\ \dfrac{1}{\varepsilon}(\varepsilon + \phi(x) - y)f, \text{ if } (x,y) \in B_1 \\ \dfrac{1}{\varepsilon}(\varepsilon - \psi(x) + y)f, \text{ if } (x,y) \in B_2 \\ \qquad 0 \qquad , \text{ if } (x,y) \in C_1 \cup C_2. \end{cases}$$

It is easy to verify that f^* is continuous in R; indeed there are no inconsistencies on the boundary between any two regions. For example, on the arc $y = \phi(x)$, $f = f^*$ as in D and, on the arc $y = \phi(x) + \varepsilon$, $f^* = 0$ as in C_1. In fact, the discontinuities of f_D have been smoothed out across the bands B_1 and B_2. The area of B_1 is given by

$$|B_1| = \int_a^b \{\phi + \varepsilon - \phi\}dx = \int_a^b \varepsilon \, dx = \varepsilon(b - a), \qquad (1)$$

and similarly

$$|B_2| = \varepsilon(b - a). \qquad (2)$$

It follows from our assumption that f is bounded, say

$$|f| \leqslant M \text{ in } D,$$

and this implies that f^* is bounded by the same number, because the factors $\dfrac{1}{\varepsilon}(\varepsilon + \phi(x) - y)$ and $\dfrac{1}{\varepsilon}(\varepsilon - \psi(x) + y)$ have values between 0 and 1 in the regions B_1 and B_2 respectively. We may therefore state that

$$|f^*| \leqslant M \text{ in } R.$$

APPENDIX

Now compare the integrals of f^* and f. Clearly

$$\iint_R f^* = \iint_D f + \iint_{B_1} f^* + \iint_{B_2} f^* + \iint_{C_1} f^* + \iint_{C_2} f^*.$$

The last two integrals are zero, since f^* vanishes in C_1 and C_2. On using (1) and (2) we find that

$$\left| \iint_{B_1} f^* \right| \leqslant \varepsilon M(b-a), \left| \iint_{B_2} f^* \right| \leqslant \varepsilon M(b-a).$$

Thus

$$\left| \iint_R f^* - \iint_D f \right| \leqslant 2\varepsilon M(b-a). \tag{3}$$

Next, by Theorem 1,

$$\iint_R f^* = \int_a^b dx \int_\alpha^\beta f^* dy = \int_a^b dx \int_{\psi-\varepsilon}^\psi f^* dy$$
$$+ \int_a^b dx \int_\psi^\phi f \, dy + \int_a^b dx \int_\phi^{\phi+\varepsilon} f^* dy,$$

where the inner integral has been broken up corresponding to the segments in which the vertical line with abscissa x meets the various subregions. We recall that $f^* = 0$ when $\alpha \leqslant y \leqslant \psi - \varepsilon$ and $\phi + \varepsilon \leqslant y \leqslant \beta$ and that $f^* = f$ when $\psi \leqslant y \leqslant \phi$. Since

$$\left| \int_a^b dx \int_{\psi-\varepsilon}^\psi f^* dy \right| \leqslant \int_a^b dx \int_{\psi-\varepsilon}^\psi M \, dy = M \int_a^b \varepsilon \, dx = M\varepsilon(b-a)$$

and similarly,

$$\left| \int_a^b dx \int_\phi^{\phi+\varepsilon} f^* dy \right| \leqslant M\varepsilon(b-a),$$

we infer that

$$\left| \iint_R f^* - \int_a^b dx \int_\varphi^\phi f \, dy \right| \leqslant 2M\varepsilon(b-a). \tag{4}$$

101

Combining the inequalities (3) and (4) we deduce that

$$\left| \iint_D f - \int_a^b dx \int_\varphi^\phi f \, dy \right| \leqslant 4M\varepsilon(b-a).$$

Since the right-hand side can be made arbitrary small, the two expressions on the left are in fact equal. This proves the assertion.

Solutions to Exercises

Chapter I

1. $x = t^2, y = t^3 \ (-1 \leqslant t \leqslant 1)$.
2. $x = t^2 \ (-1 \leqslant t \leqslant 1)$ and $x = 1 \ (1 \leqslant t \leqslant 2)$; $y = t \ (-1 \leqslant t \leqslant 1)$ and $y = 3 - 2t \ (1 \leqslant t \leqslant 2)$.
3. $(5\sqrt{5} - 1)/12$.
4. $8\sinh^{-1}1$.
5. $2\log 2 - 1$.
6. Let $P = \int p \, dx$, $Q = \int q \, dy$, $f = P + Q$ and use equation (8) on p. 11.
8. The function $\tan^{-1}(y/x)$ is not single-valued.
9. $2\pi(a^2 + \pi b^2)$.
11. Rotate the axes so as to bring the equation of the ellipse into the normal form $(\lambda\xi)^2 + (\mu\eta)^2 = 1$ and observe that the area is $\pi/\lambda\mu$.
12. $4ab/3$.

Chapter II

1. $\pi a^4/4$.
2. $\sin y$.
3. The region of integration is the triangle with vertices $(0,0)$, $(\pi/2, \pi/2)$, $(0, \pi/2)$.
4. The rule for interchanging the order of integration does not apply, because the integrand has a singularity at $(0,0)$.
5. The region of integration is bounded by the parabola $y^2 = ax$ and the straight line $y = x$.
6. $a^3(3\pi - 4)/9$.
7. Use (43), p. 55. ANS.: $(ab)^{-1}$.
8. Put $u = x^2 - y^2$, $v = xy$; ANS.: $3/4$.
9. Put $u = x^2 + 2y^2$, $v = y/x$. ANS.: $2^{-\frac{3}{2}}\{\tan^{-1}2\sqrt{2} - \tan^{-1}\frac{1}{2}\sqrt{2}\}$.

SOLUTIONS TO EXERCISES

10. Change to polar coordinates; the ensuing integral

$$\int_0^{\pi/2} (1 + \cos \alpha \sin 2\theta)^{-1} d\theta$$

may be evaluated by putting $t = \tan \theta$.

11. 84.

12. $128a^3/15$.

13. Region of integration: $x^2 + y^2 \leqslant 15a^2/16$; boundary surfaces: $z = (a^2 - x^2 - y^2)^{\frac{1}{2}}$, $z = 2a - (4a^2 - x^2 - y^2)^{\frac{1}{2}}$. ANS.: $13\pi^3/24$.

14. $a^2b(9\pi - 16)/36$.

15. Take for region of integration $x^2 + y^2 \leqslant a^2$; on account of symmetry it suffices to consider the portion for which $0 \leqslant y \leqslant x$, where the bounding surfaces are $z = \pm (a^2 - x^2)^{\frac{1}{2}}$. ANS.: $16a^3(1 - 2^{-\frac{1}{2}})$.

Chapter III

2. The two surfaces intersect in a curve whose projection on the (x,y)-plane are the lines $x + y - a = 0$ and $x + y + a = 0$ (eliminate z). Since $z^2 = 2xy$ passes through the lines $x = 0$ and $y = 0$, the region of integration is the union of the triangles with vertices (0.0), $(a,0)$, $(0,a)$ and $(0,0)$, $(-a,0)$, $(0,-a)$ respectively. Use II, (43). ANS.: $\sqrt{2}\pi a^2$.

3. $4\pi^2ab$.

4. $4\pi a^4/3$. Observe that, by symmetry,

$$\iint_S x^2 dS = \iint_S y^2 dS = \iint_S z^2 dS.$$

5. $37\pi/10$.

6. Note that $(a^2 - 2ap + p^2)^{\frac{1}{2}} = |a \pm p|$.

Chapter IV

1. 2.

2. Put $x = a\xi$, $y = b\eta$, $z = c\zeta$ and then use polar coordinates. ANS.: $4\pi abc(e - 2)$.

3. Put $\xi = x - a$, $\eta = y - a$, $\zeta = z - a$. Note that the integral of an odd power of ξ or η or ζ over the interior of the sphere $\xi^2 + \eta^2 + \zeta^2 = 1$ is zero. ANS.: $32\pi a^6/5$.

SOLUTIONS TO EXERCISES

6. By symmetry reduce the region to the positive octant, then put $x = a\xi^{\frac{1}{2}}$, $y = b\eta^{\frac{1}{2}}$, $z = c\zeta^{\frac{1}{2}}$ and use Dirichlet's formula (exercise 4). ANS.: $4\pi(abc)^3/945$.

7. Use the formulae $px = a^2 \cos \alpha$, ... of p. 88 and apply the divergence theorem (p. 86).

9. Use spherical polar coordinates. After integration with respect to ϕ and θ, the integral reduces to $2\pi \int_0^a \frac{r}{\rho}\{r + \rho - |\rho - r|\}dr$ (care is needed when $\rho < a$).

11. $k = 2$.

12. Apply the divergence theorem.

Index